For my grandchildren Nina, Gavriil, and Marfa,
who might live to see the twenty-second century

Russia

Dmitri Trenin

Polity

The right of Dmitri Trenin to be identified as Author of this Work has been asserted in accordance with the UK Copyright, Designs and Patents Act 1988.

First published in 2019 by Polity Press
Reprinted 2019 (twice)

Polity Press
65 Bridge Street
Cambridge CB2 1UR, UK

Polity Press
101 Station Landing
Suite 300
Medford, MA 02155, USA

ISBN-13: 978-1-5095-2766-3
ISBN-13: 978-1-5095-2767-0 (pbk)

A catalogue record for this book is available from the British Library.

Library of Congress Cataloging-in-Publication Data
Names: Trenin, Dmitriĭ, author.
Title: Russia / Dmitri Trenin.
Description: Medford, MA : Polity Press, 2019. | Series: Polity histories | Includes bibliographical references and index.
Identifiers: LCCN 2018061779 (print) | LCCN 2019001303 (ebook) | ISBN 9781509527700 (Epub) | ISBN 9781509527663 (hardback) | ISBN 9781509527670 (pbk.)
Subjects: LCSH: Soviet Union--History. | Russia (Federation)--History--1991-
Classification: LCC DK266 (ebook) | LCC DK266 .T655 2019 (print) | DDC 947.084--dc23
LC record available at https://lccn.loc.gov/2018061779

Typeset in 11 on 13 Berkeley by Servis Filmsetting Ltd, Stockport, Cheshire
Printed and bound in the United States by LSC Communication

For further information on Polity, visit our website: politybooks.com

Contents

Map	vi
Preface	vii
Acknowledgments	ix
Introduction: Russia's Many Russias	1
1 Revolutionary Upheaval (1900–20)	16
2 The Rise of the Soviet State (1921–38)	51
3 World War II and Its Aftermath (1939–52)	77
4 Mature Socialism and Its Stagnation (1953–84)	100
5 Democratic Upheaval (1985–99)	122
6 From Stability to Uncertainty (2000–19)	149
Conclusion: Forever Russia	177
Further Reading	186
Notes	190
Index	193

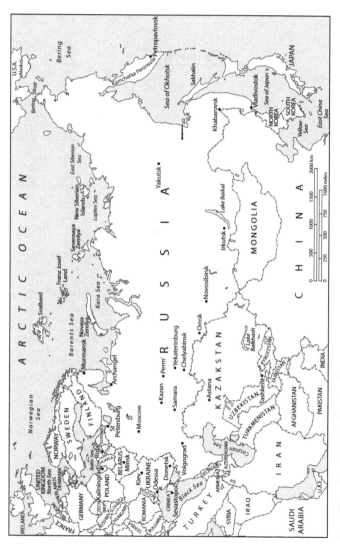

Map of Russia and Its Neighborhood

Preface

This short book is not an academic treatise. It does not pretend to reveal archival discoveries, or advance some intricate new theory of Russian history. Nor is it a textbook for students of Russia. Rather, it is an introduction to modern Russian history written for a non-Russian, non-specialist audience.

With this in mind, my purpose is simple and straightforward: to help readers understand where Russia is coming from. In other words, I will attempt to unravel the logic of the country's history to make sense of its earlier development and its contemporary behavior, and what might be expected of it in the future.

Today Russia remains a highly politicized subject in the West. As someone who lives in Russia but is used to looking at his own country from the outside, I will offer an insider's perspective that recognizes Russia's current image as mostly negative or controversial and often baffling, whilst going beyond the usual clichés to describe a "Russians' Russia." By this I mean the way people – from ordinary men and women to prominent figures and leaders – went about their daily lives, engaged in their private or collective endeavors, experienced and engaged in politics, and, occasionally, made history.

Sergiev Posad, February 11, 2019

Acknowledgments

This book was, to me, a particularly difficult undertaking. Compressing into a tight 45,000-word-long text my own country's 120 years of history – four revolutions, two world wars, a bloody domestic civil war and a cold foreign one, with several dizzying and terrifying transformations along the way, steep rises and stunning falls, followed by a comeback offering an uncertain future – was a huge challenge. I naturally hesitated, but in the end was persuaded by my Polity editor, Dr. Louise Knight, to try to rise to the occasion. Louise also encouraged me, and helped me considerably to improve my original draft. I want to thank Sophie Wright for guiding me through the process of book editing. For very careful editing of the text, I am indebted to Justin Dyer. My esteemed colleague William J. Burns, President of the Carnegie Endowment for International Peace in Washington, DC, and a former US Ambassador to Russia, has read the manuscript and commented on it, for which I am most grateful. I am also deeply thankful to my family: my wife Vera, who looked at me with understanding when I holed up in my study at weekends; my elder son Petr, a trained historian with a Moscow University degree, who read the draft most closely, and supplied numerous questions and criticisms, as well as pages of suggestions; and my younger son Andrei, who urged me never to give up.

Introduction:
Russia's Many Russias

The Russia of the Communist period has often been
derided as a country with an unpredictable history.
This is true, of course, particularly in relation to the
recounting of history in official Soviet propaganda
and school textbooks. There, important facts, usually from the recent past, were denied as if they had
never existed, and others were grossly distorted,
while all-powerful leaders, once disgraced, could end
up as non-persons overnight – all to suit the current
demands of the new party leadership. My parents-in-
law kept a complete set of the second edition of the
Grand Soviet Encyclopaedia. One day, I found inserted
in volume 2, which was published in 1950,[1] several
loose pages with a note sent by the publisher (some-
time in 1953 or shortly thereafter). The note asked
the owners of the volume to tear out the pages con-
taining the biography of Stalin's secret police chief
Lavrentiy Beria and replace them with the readily
supplied new pages, which contained no entry on
him. Touchingly, the note even instructed the book
owners how to do this carefully without damaging
the book. My in-laws never did what they had been
asked to do, but they kept the note and the extra
pages in the book next to the portrait of the disgraced

Stalinist monster – as a relic of one of the zigzags of Soviet history.

Russia is hardly unique in letting its leaders play with history to legitimize their rule, to claim a special status in world affairs, or to indicate a future trajectory. Today, "history politics" is on rich display in a number of countries, from post-Communist Eastern Europe to post-Soviet Ukraine, the Caucasus, and Central Asia: all nation-building is essentially an exercise in myth-making. In Russia, the job, as it turns out, is never complete, as a function of the constant search for the "right" vector of development. A fresh attempt at this is under way even as you read these lines. Don't get me wrong: serious historical research has always existed in Russia. Here, I discuss "history politics" as the use of the past to legitimize the present and chart one's way into the future.

This is not merely an exercise in political expediency. Russia stands out as a country that has had to constantly reinvent itself. Whenever an existential crisis arrived, Russia virtually turned against its own past, creating monumental discontinuities in its historical path. Thus, there are clear and seemingly unbridgeable divides between heathen and Christian Russia; the pre-Mongol "Kievan" ("European") period and Moscow's "gathering of Russian lands" under the Golden Horde's Asian empire; the Orthodox Muscovite tsardom and the Westernized empire of St. Petersburg; and, of course, between imperial, Soviet, and contemporary Russias. At any given moment, the country's way forward is informed by what its leaders and the bulk of the people consider to be the "true," "bedrock" Russia.

Yet, paradoxically, *plus ça change, plus c'est la même chose*. There is a bedrock. They say that in Russia everything changes in 20 years, and nothing in 200. This points to a remarkable resilience of some of the core features of the nation's existence, its self-image, and its worldview. Russia is like a phoenix: it repeatedly turns to ashes only to be reborn in some new guise. The key to understanding these transformations lies in the Russian people's collective experience.

The Birth of Russian Exceptionalism

As just noted, over the course of its millennium-long history, "Russia" has gone through a number of incarnations. It first emerged in the mid-ninth century as a Viking-governed union of Slavic tribes covering a vast area of Europe's east, from Novgorod in the north to Kiev in the south. What later became known as Kievan Rus was an eastern version of Charlemagne's empire, very much part of medieval Europe's political set-up, and a common birthplace of present-day Russia, Ukraine, and Belarus. All three countries rightly claim the whole of this historical legacy, but none can claim it as exclusively its own. The most important lasting achievement of that first version of this European-born Russia remains Orthodox Christianity, which it embraced from Constantinople in 988.

Kievan Rus lasted longer than Charlemagne's realm, but it, too, eventually fragmented into a collection of feudal principalities ruled by a single large family. Kiev first became a coveted prize, and then lost political significance. In the early thirteenth century, Russian lands were invaded and quickly overrun by the Mongols. Mongol rule was subsequently established in the north-east of the country, which now forms the nucleus of the Russian Federation. Russians living in that area spent the following 250 years within the great Asian empire built by Genghis Khan. By contrast, western (now Belarus) and south-western (Ukraine) principalities were incorporated into Lithuania, Hungary, and later Poland.

The implications of this division were crucial. North-eastern Russians lost their independence and their contacts with the West, but kept their religion. For these Russians, the principal takeaways from the trying period were the mortal danger of political disunity and the unifying nature of Orthodox Christianity. By contrast, western and south-western Russians, having escaped Mongol rule, formed Orthodox minorities within the predominantly Catholic countries of Eastern Europe. They never recovered political independence, but some of them became integrated into the social order of the Polish–Lithuanian Commonwealth. This split of the early Russian nation has produced different political cultures and outlooks in Russia, on one hand, and Ukraine and Belarus, on the other.

Rebirth of an independent Russian state was championed by Moscow, initially a tiny town on a small river whose rise owed a lot to the entrepreneurship, thriftiness, cunning, and ruthlessness of its dukes. Physically unprotected on the great Eastern European plain, they constantly faced danger from all corners and had to be able to mobilize for defense quickly. Strategically, these dukes followed the behest of Alexander Nevsky, a mid-thirteenth-century Novgorod prince, who, wedged between the German crusaders and the Mongol hordes, chose to fight the former and accommodate the latter. His rationale was that paying tribute to foreigners and accepting their suzerainty – i.e., losing the country's body – was preferable to the abandonment of Orthodoxy and conversion to Catholicism – i.e., losing the people's soul.

The choice was hard, but it proved right. It was the Orthodox Church that, from the fourteenth century, became the spiritual guide of national revival in Russia's north-east. It was then that the Moscow dukes managed to make their town the seat of the metropolitan of all Russia, who heretofore had sat in Kiev. Political and spiritual unity, echoing the Byzantine harmony of the emperor and the patriarch, and Alexander Nevsky's geopolitical choice have since become key features of "Russianness."

By the late fifteenth century, Moscow's rulers had again "reinvented" Russia. Grand Duke Ivan III managed to found the first unified Russian state. Not only did he reassemble disparate principalities of the north-east under a centralized state, he also overthrew the "Mongol yoke." In a historic reversal, Moscow's rulers would soon overtake the former, mostly Turkic khanates of the disintegrated Golden Horde and absorb them into the new Russian state, also allowing the new Muslim subjects to keep their religion, and letting their nobles join the Russian ruling class as equals. Such integration later became the method of the Russian Empire. The Russians also adopted an authoritarian political culture that made their state strong and their people subservient to it.

But that was not all. After the fall of the Byzantine Empire to the Ottoman Turks in the mid-fifteenth century, Moscow claimed spiritual leadership of the entire Orthodox world, as a "Third Rome" – after Rome itself and Constantinople. Coming from the same dynasty as the old Kievan princes, the Moscow grand dukes also claimed all the lands of the former Kievan Rus as their patrimony. Symbolically, Russia adopted the Byzantine double-headed eagle as its coat of arms and the "Monomach cap" as its rulers' crown, so called after the last prince of unified Kievan Rus. In the mid-sixteenth century, Moscow's Duke Ivan IV promoted himself to tsar – i.e., caesar – and a few decades later the metropolitans of Moscow and all Russia became patriarchs. Thus, they put themselves on a par with the Holy Roman emperors and the patriarchs of Constantinople. Accepting no higher authority in the world, whether temporal or religious, has since lain at the foundation of Russia's brand of exceptionalism. Alongside the authoritarian political culture, this became deeply entrenched in the Russian psyche.

"Moscow Rus," or "Muscovy," as it became known, went through the Time of Troubles in the early seventeenth century, brought about by the end of the dynasty that had founded Kievan Rus; fought off an attempt by neighboring Poland to take it over; established a new dynasty, the Romanovs; added eastern Ukraine to the realm; and experienced a most traumatic religious schism within the Orthodoxy. In many ways, however, Russia was lagging behind its neighbors in Europe. In 1700, its modernizing monarch, Tsar Peter I, sought to gain direct access to the Baltic Sea to be able to trade with the advanced countries of Western Europe. In order to achieve this, Peter started a war with Sweden, which controlled the Baltic shores. The long war endowed Russia with a modern state structure and turned it into a great European power, with a capital in St. Petersburg, a city built from scratch, amid Baltic swamps. Westernization became the thrust of the government's policy.

The Russian Empire lasted almost 200 years. It expanded to include a wide swath of land in Eastern Europe, Central Asia, and the Caucasus, and the Far East. It thwarted Napoleon's invasion and became an indispensable element of the Concert of Europe and the global balance of power. It began to modernize late, essentially after the abolition of serfdom in 1861, but by the early twentieth century was developing at a fast pace. It produced a long line of world-class writers, poets, composers, and ballet dancers. However, Russia's European façade and its huge, very traditional backyard remained at odds with each other. Its staunchly conservative political system stifled freedom and bred some of the most radical opposition elements, from Nihilist terrorists to Bolsheviks. And the center was too weak. Like during the Time of Troubles three centuries before, the loss of control by the top leadership spelled disaster. Nicholas II, Russia's last emperor, a respectable family man, turned out a complete failure as a leader. The result was the 1917 revolution that totally destroyed the regime, the system, the state, and the country. Soon a new state was born: it was the Soviet Union, which saw its predecessor as a class enemy.

Like the Russian Empire, the Soviet Union was not doomed to fall when it did. Yet, as with Nicholas II, the loss of control by Mikhail Gorbachev spelled its fate. Three decades on, however, the Russian Federation looks less like a "new Russia," signifying another clean break with the past, than a continuation state of the Soviet Union, the Russian Empire, and the tsardom of Muscovy. This inclusivity is new, and it means neither indifference nor moral relativism. The Russian people, imagined as a national jury, are still in the process of passing judgment not only about their leaders and the regimes they instituted or represented, but also about themselves. Questions such as "Who are we?" and "Where do we belong?" are once more on the agenda. History supplies a major part of the answer.

Recurring Features

What stands out from this briefest possible outline is that Russia is a succession of states and represents the continuity of a country. Russia periodically changes its "garb," but each time it retains some key features.

To begin with, there has been strong rejection of any form of dependence on outside powers and simultaneous acquiescence in often harsh authoritarian rule at home. In other words, Russian people take pride in the sovereign freedom of their state in the international arena while they are willing to forfeit their own domestic sovereignty vis-à-vis that same state. It is the state with power vested in its titular head that has dominated the Russian nation. Not only the rulers, but even most ordinary people regard it as the supreme national value. Indeed, it is the common state, rather than ethnicity or religion, that unites Russian people. The collapse of the state, which has happened three times in the last 400 years, lets loose demons which are considered worse than authoritarianism.

Russia also demonstrates a high degree of physical connectivity, while remaining essentially lonely. To the west, in Europe and more recently in the United States, Russia has faced socially and politically different and technologically advanced countries, which it regards as both main external sources of modernization and geopolitical competitors; in Asia to the east, it faces civilizations even more different from its own than those of the West; to the south lies the Muslim world, elements of which Russia has managed to integrate within the country, but whose rumblings make it feel vulnerable.

Russians have an ambivalent attitude toward the country's place in the world and among other peoples: Is Russia part of Europe or is it apart from Europe? If it is Eurasia, what does this mean, precisely? Is it a great power on a par with the strongest in the world, or is it simply a big and rather backward country with outsize ambitions? The trouble is that none of these questions has a clear finite answer. Russia is European, but it is not part of Europe. If anything, it is a part of the world. Its geography and sheer size – 11 time zones – have been both a blessing and a curse. The distinction between "Europe" and "Asia" within Russia is blurred: de Gaulle's famous phrase about a "Europe from the Atlantic to the Urals" never made sense there. And, in order to stay in the power game, Russia has always had to punch above its weight.

Russia demonstrates its own version of exceptionalism. From the Third Rome of Orthodoxy to the Third International of Communism, religious faith or its secular equivalent was central to it. When the idea weakened and waned, that had dire implications for the state and the nation. "Saintly Russia" first eroded from within, before it drowned in the revolutions and wars of the early twentieth century; and Communist Russia, hollowed out by the real experience of the Soviet Union, went down with a whimper toward the end of the same fateful century.

Unbroken Whole

This book treats Russia's history as an unbroken whole. It does not pretend that the Russian Federation is a different country to the Soviet Union and the Russian Empire, or that the Soviet Union was just a painful aberration to be treated separately from the rest of Russian history. As a Russian who was 36 when the Communist system collapsed, and served in the Soviet military at the time, the author naturally acknowledges that *the Soviet Union was us.* The USSR was an important chapter in the 1,250-year-long history of Russian statehood; in that history, it is anything but a "lost" period. The book also takes a broad look at the Russian past. It does not limit itself to political developments only, although it focuses on them; it also looks at Russia's economy, society, ideology, and culture to give a comprehensive picture of a country through one of its most trying, and often tragic, periods of existence.

Each of the six chapters that follow covers on average 20 years of history. The first, spanning 1900 to 1920, deals with the revolutionary upheaval of the early twentieth century and its aftermath. It describes a vibrant economy, unstable society, static autocracy, and a state-run Orthodox Church increasingly distant from society: the basic ingredients of Russia's revolution. It addresses the spiritual sources of revolution, first described by Fyodor Dostoevsky in his 1872 novel *The Demons*. The chapter looks at Russia's first

battle in the twentieth century: the unfortunate war
with Japan and the first Russian revolution. It passes
through the charming but decadent Silver Age culture
before plunging the reader into World War I, the prime
catalyst of the violent change to come. It seeks to make
sense of the revolutionary developments of 1917,
from the fall of the Romanov dynasty in February to
the Bolshevik takeover in October. Finally, the chapter
seeks to understand the reasons for the Reds' victory
in the Civil War and for the restoration – albeit in a
very different form – of a centralized state covering
most of the territory of the Russian Empire.

The second chapter (1921–38) examines the rise
of Soviet socialism as a totalitarian system with its
salient political, economic, and social features. In particular, it looks at political unification under a single
monolithic party and its bureaucratization; economic
industrialization; collectivization, which was in fact
a war on the peasantry; official atheism and the war
on religion; as well as mass repression on a gigantic
scale and the emergence of the GULAG. It discusses
the cultural revolution and the birth of socialist realism, which was the dominant ideology in the arts,
in addition to the tragedy of traditional Russian culture inside the country and the Russian emigration
abroad.

Chapter 3 (1939–52) discusses the run-up to the
Great Patriotic War, the war itself, and post-war reconstruction. It pays particular attention to Moscow's foreign policy and diplomacy and its prosecution of the

war. It features the behavior of the Soviet people in the period of ultimate trial, and seeks to understand the sources of their resilience and of the Soviet victory in World War II. In its treatment of the post-war period, the chapter looks at the origins of the Cold War from a Russian perspective. It also covers the final years of Stalin's rule.

The fourth chapter is devoted to the Soviet system in its three decades of maturity, from 1953 till 1984. This was the Soviet Union as it is still remembered by the living generations. Very limited political liberalization replaced totalitarianism with a brand of authoritarianism. Economic and technological development at first spurred ahead, but having exhausted the easily available resources, and unable to reform due to rigid ideology, it stagnated. Political stability, initially a welcome change from the perennial purges and repressions of the previous period, eventually led to gerontocracy. The tremendous prestige won as a result of World War II was converted into geopolitical dominance in Eurasia, but insistence on absolute control eroded that system from the inside, and imperial overstretch to the four corners of the world undermined it from the outside. The supreme achievement of the era, strategic parity with the United States, required a degree of militarization of the Soviet economy that plunged it into crisis. By the mid-1980s, the Soviet Union was in deep trouble.

Chapter 5 deals with the new time of troubles, from 1985 through 1999. One important question posed in this chapter is whether the Soviet system was reformable during this period. A definite answer is probably not available, but an analysis of the policies of perestroika and glasnost suggests that those policies, within a few short years, made any successful reform impossible. A total collapse followed – of the Communist power system and the Soviet Union itself; of the Soviet economy and its technological capacity; of science and culture; and, not least, of the societal morals, norms, and values. The up-side was sudden freedom – of speech, movement, entrepreneurship, religion, but essentially without law and order. Another major question that this chapter seeks to understand is the reasons for the failure of political democracy in Russia and of the country's integration into the expanding West.

The final chapter of this book must remain open-ended. It begins on January 1, 2000, the first full day of Vladimir Putin's presidency, and will naturally end with Putin's abdication from supreme power in Russia. In 2019, this still seems a long way off. Coming to the Kremlin after the period of upheaval, Putin was above all a stabilizer. His (so far) almost two decades in power have been a period of relative peace, prosperity, and personal freedom. Putin has restored order, and created the belief that the Russian state is back. He has managed to keep the country in one piece, and it has the clout of a great power once more – albeit at the cost of a confrontation with the United States. Putin has become the godfather of contemporary Russian capitalism, with its state corporations, tame tycoons, and crass inequality. Yet he is also a transitional figure. The regime that he has built will probably not survive after he is gone.

The secret of Putin's Russia is that it is a regime posing as a state. Installing a regime in place of chaos was a big step forward in the 2000s, but this is not enough. Contemporary Russia is very un-Russian. It has few things that are common to all its people. Money has become its central organizing principle. This frees the elites from any responsibility and accountability, even to the head of the regime. There are no informal rules that apply to all, only conventions as in criminal societies. In most advanced countries, people get rich before joining government or civil service and after they leave it. In Russia, most wealthy people enrich themselves while in government, or thanks to their links to it. Such a system is inimical to any values, norms, principles, solidarity, national ideas, and the like. Nor is it is sustainable in the long term. The issue is how, by whom, when, and by what it is replaced. For all these questions, to be raised in the Conclusion, there is ample food for thought in the main body of the book.

The journey begins. Welcome aboard.

1

Revolutionary Upheaval
(1900–20)

Russia entered the twentieth century as the largest country in the world after the British Empire, covering about one-sixth of the globe's surface. The Russian emperor's full title ran to dozens of lines. His realm included all the territories now belonging to the Russian Federation (except for Kaliningrad, then the northern part of East Prussia); Ukraine (minus Galicia and Volynia, then under Austro-Hungarian rule); Belarus; most of Poland; the whole of Finland, Estonia, Latvia, and Lithuania; all of Moldova, Georgia, Armenia, Azerbaijan, and part of eastern Turkey; and the entire territories of Kazakhstan, Uzbekistan, Tajikistan, Kyrgyzstan, and Turkmenistan. Alaska, a Russian possession, had been sold to the United States in 1867. However, the Russian sphere of influence extended even further: to Mongolia and Manchuria in China's north and north-east, where the Russians had just founded a major city, Harbin, and leased a naval base in Port Arthur on the Yellow Sea; to eastern Turkestan, now Chinese Xinjiang; and to northern Persia with Tehran. This enormous contiguous territory covering two-fifths of Eurasia's landmass formed the geographical basis of Russian power.

Population and Governance

In terms of population, Russia, with its 129 million people, according to the 1897 census,[1] was bigger than any country in the world except for China and (then British) India, and growing rapidly. Ethnically, the population of such a huge empire had to be very diverse. Ethnic Russians ("great Russians") accounted for only 44.3%, but they were bundled together with the Ukrainians ("little Russians," 17.8%) and the Belarusians (4.7%) as the Orthodox "Russian people," who still held a two-thirds majority among the tsar's subjects. Other major ethnic groups included the Poles (6.3%), Jews (4.1%, the world's largest community at the time), Germans (1.4%), and various Turkic-speaking peoples: Tatars, Bashkirs, Kazakhs, Uzbeks, Kyrgyz, and others (10.8%). These groups were held together by religious tradition (70% considered themselves Orthodox Christians, as opposed to 9% Muslims, 9% Catholics, 5% Lutherans, and 4% Jewish),[2] the scepter of the tsar and his sword. As nationalism was spreading in Europe and beyond, it was only a matter of time before at least some of these groups would claim nationhood and statehood.

Russia was the only absolute monarchy in Europe. When filling out his 1897 census questionnaire, Nicholas II, who had ascended the throne three years earlier, gave his occupation as "the master of the Russian land." Russia still had no parliament. Its State Council, composed largely of noblemen, was an advisory body to the emperor. The Committee of Ministers was not a real cabinet, with each of its members reporting directly to the tsar, who personally made all major decisions at the state level. The dozens of provinces across the empire were administered on the monarch's behalf by the governors whom he appointed. The judiciary system operated on a body of laws and a jury system was in practice, but the judges were all appointed. Only local government – *zemstvas* and city dumas – was partially in the hands of elected members of society, but their prerogatives were narrow. On a daily basis, the country was run by the bureaucracy. The empire, however, allowed for some flexibility. Finland, officially a Grand Duchy, enjoyed a parliament, as well as a monetary system and a police force of its own. At the other extreme, the emirs of Bukhara and the khans of Khiva were allowed to continue with their medieval forms of governance.

After Peter I had abolished the patriarchy in 1700, the Russian Orthodox Church, the dominant religious organization, was administered by a Synod overseen by an officer whom the tsar appointed. In the nineteenth century and at the beginning of the twentieth, the Russian church was not going through the best of times. With the emperor as its de facto head, and the clergy on the government's payroll, the church, confined to its gilded cage, was increasingly regarded as another department of the state. In these conditions it could not become a moral force. With the church deprived of freedom, the prestige of the bishops and priests sank, with many of them seen as too worldly, and sometimes immoral. This erosion of religious faith among both the ordinary people and the cultured elites would have tragic consequences in the years ahead.

A hereditary autocrat, Nicholas II rejected as "mindless dreams" any suggestion of a representative government, not to mention political rights guaranteed by a constitution. In that, he followed the example of his father, Alexander III, who vowed to strengthen autocratic rule after revolutionary terrorists assassinated his own father Alexander II in 1881. Nicholas II's highest ambition was, in due course, to hand over full autocratic powers, intact, to his own successor. This stubborn insistence on the integrity of absolute monarchy at the beginning of the twentieth century proved fatal. The tsar turned out to be ill equipped for the enormous task he faced as his empire entered trying times.

The Estates

The Russian tsar was the country's first nobleman. In 1913, the Romanov family marked its tricentennial anniversary on the Russian throne. The tsars had always relied on the gentry, who were expected to serve them in war and peace, to be compensated for that with land and the peasants who worked on it. From 1649, the peasants lost the right to move and were bound to a particular estate and its owner, thus becoming serfs. In 1762, the nobles were freed from obligatory service to the emperor. This freedom contributed to a spectacular rise of Russian high culture – particularly literature and music – but it also led to the decline of the sense of duty and even the morals of the noblemen, many of whom chose to remain completely idle in their estates or abroad.

In 1861, as part of a major reform effort by Alexander II, the serfs were at last given personal freedom. By 1900, the role of the Russian gentry, who accounted for about 1.5% of the population, had diminished dramatically. Next to free labor, they lost about half of the land they used to own. They had to make room for much more energetic groups: rich peasants-turned-capitalists, merchants-turned-entrepreneurs, and the rising bourgeois intelligentsia. Even though many nobles still held important positions in the civil administration and in the military, quite a few became disoriented, and were satirized in plays by Chekhov, such as *Uncle Vanya* (1899) and *The Cherry Orchard* (1904). In many ways, the 1917 revolution in Russia was a day of reckoning for the centuries of oppression of the peasants by the landed gentry.

At the beginning of the twentieth century, Russia was still a largely peasant society. Peasants constituted 86% of Russia's population. They owned 62% of all arable land, against 22% still held by the gentry. However, 83% of that land was owned collectively, so individual peasants could neither sell nor buy land on which they worked.[3] Every dozen years or so, land was reassigned within the community, depending on the size of the families. It is hardly a coincidence that years of land reapportionment – 1905, 1917 – also happened to be the years of revolution in Russia. The Land Question was compounded by the fact that while Russia possessed some of the best soils in the world, its agriculture was primitive, and the ownership structure did not stimulate entrepreneurship. Though the country exported much grain, bad harvests frequently led to food shortages domestically.

Many peasants migrated to the cities, where industry was experiencing rapid growth. Yet by the beginning of the twentieth century, industrial workers were still a small social group. Of the 13–14 million hired workers, fewer than 3 million were employed at industrial enterprises. Workers' power, however, lay not so much in their numbers as in their concentration in the major cities. In a highly centralized country, this was a serious advantage. The workers were also much easier to mobilize by a political force who would win their hearts and minds. The Bolsheviks understood this better than anyone. The Workers' Question was fast coming to the fore.

The Russian bourgeoisie, its roots in the merchant class, did not really emerge until the nineteenth century, but grew rapidly in its second half. By the turn of the twentieth century, entrepreneurs numbered about 1.5 million,[4] but few of them were making much money. Russian traditional culture did not look kindly on people making money. Often, they were regarded as "predators." Even though a number of successful industrialists, bankers, and merchants managed to get very rich, they developed few political ambitions and their influence on decision-making was very limited. Many preferred philanthropy – paying society back for their success.

The intelligentsia – a special group of educated people who worked for hire – was very much a Russian feature, as was the word itself. In the second half of the nineteenth century, many members of that group, from university students to literary types, fancied themselves representatives of the common people – still mostly illiterate – in the face of the tsarist regime, which they saw as oppressive and unjust. Initially they "went to the people," as the phrase went, and became country teachers, doctors, vets, and the like. Over time, they became radicalized and sought to revolutionize the peasants. Some formed terrorist organizations. Fyodor Dostoevsky vividly – and unsympathetically – described them in *The Demons*. By the turn of the twentieth century, the more radical part of the intelligentsia defined itself through civic and moral responsibility. Its members saw their mission as being society's consciousness. That meant principled opposition to the state and its institutions.

Culture

Russian philosophy is not particularly well known outside the country, but the turn of the twentieth century saw it in full blossom. An influential collection of articles called *Vekhi* (Milestones) criticized liberal radicalism and proposed a conservative alternative. Religious thinkers like Vladimir Solovyov, Nikolai Berdyaev, Sergei Bulgakov, and others sought to synthesize Orthodoxy, Greek and modern German philosophy. Their views strengthened the universalist, essentially global dimension of Russian thought. Orthodox philosophy is also linked to Russian "cosmism," or cosmic philosophy, best represented by the scientists Konstantin Tsiolkovsky and Vladimir Vernadsky, but it also had an occultist branch led by Mme. Blavatsky. A distinct feature of Russian philosophy is that it is rooted in Orthodoxy rather than in the Renaissance.

At the turn of the twentieth century, Russian culture was entering what became known as its "Silver Age," after the golden one of the century before. However, the dissimilarities between the two ages were also striking. The nineteenth-century giants – Pushkin, Gogol, Turgenev, Dostoevsky, Tolstoy – were above all realists. They looked at life as a whole, and sought to "sow the reasonable, good, and eternal," in the words of the poet Nikolai Nekrasov. This leitmotif was taken up by the writer Anton Chekhov, Konstantin Stanislavsky's Moscow Art Theater, and then by Maxim Gorky and Ivan Bunin.

The new generation's view was anything but realist. It was fragmented, partial, and symbolic. The poets Alexander Blok and Valery Bryusov and the writer Dmitri Merezhkovsky best represented the new trend.

This reflected not only a desire to find some heretofore hidden unconventional truth, but a lot of confusion in many leading minds. Arts flourished, experimentation was rife. The Russian Silver Age gave birth to avant-garde art – pioneered by such figures as Konstantin Malevich, Marc Chagall, and Wassily Kandinsky. This most powerful world trend of the twentieth century was given a boost by the Russian revolution, but its roots were actually planted in the decade preceding it.

In the arts, impresario Sergei Diaghilev brought his *Ballets russes* to Paris; singer Feodor Shaliapin began his rise to world fame; painters Vasily Surikov, Ilya Repin, Isaak Levitan, and others came up with dozens of masterpieces that can be seen today in Moscow's Tretyakov Gallery and the Russian Museum in St. Petersburg. In the sciences, moreover, Dmitry Mendeleev (chemistry), Ivan Pavlov (physiology), and Alexander Popov (physics) were among the learned world's leading lights.

Foreign Policy

The Russian Empire was one of the established great powers. Its foreign policy sought to keep a balance among the major countries of Europe; to expand its influence in Asia; and to establish its primacy in the Near East, from the Balkans to the Turkish Straits. In a major strategic reversal, Russia in the early 1890s replaced its traditional alliance with Berlin by a new treaty with Paris. In Europe's new geopolitical combination, two flank countries, Russia and France, balanced the central powers, Germany and Austria-Hungary. Austrian and Russian interests clashed in the Balkans, where Russia regarded the Slavic Orthodox countries as allies, having brought them freedom from Ottoman rule. Russia's historical desire to take control of the Bosporus and the Dardanelles, the keys to the Black Sea, pitted it against both Germany and Great Britain.

It was the Far East, however, that saw most diplomatic and military action in the early years of the twentieth century. In 1891, Russia began building the Trans-Siberian railroad that eventually linked the European part of the empire with Vladivostok. In the late 1890s, Russian railroad construction expanded into North-East China. In 1898, Russia forced China to lease to it part of the Liaodong Peninsula, where it built a naval base and a commercial port. A clique of courtiers, driven by commercial interests, pushed Nicholas II to expand into Korea, which was also a target of Japan's colonial interest. Tokyo sought a compromise, but St. Petersburg arrogantly rejected it.

The war that began in 1904 was unfortunate for Russia. It was defeated both on land and at sea. The death toll amounted to 400,000. This came as a shock: for the first time in modern history, an Asian nation had prevailed over a European great power. Russia's huge resources were still sufficient to continue the war, but growing unrest within the country pushed the tsar to seek peace. The treaty was signed in

Portsmouth, New Hampshire, in August 1905, under which Russia lost some territory in the Far East. The tsarist regime was humiliated both within Russia and internationally. The memory of that war is kept alive in Russia in several popular songs and waltzes, such as "Varyag," "The Hills of Manchuria," and the "The Amur Waves."

Revolutionary Upheaval

With the end of the war, the government was able to turn its full attention to the increasingly unstable situation at home. Things had been deteriorating for several years. Peasant uprisings in the countryside, liberal opposition in the cities, and terrorist assassinations of government ministers made the regime look weak. In January 1905, a peaceful demonstration by workers and their families marched on the Winter Palace to present a petition to the tsar that asked for representative government and basic political freedoms. The tsar's troops opened fire: 200 people were killed, 800 wounded. The massacre dramatically radicalized the situation. "Bloody Sunday," as it came to be called, destroyed the popular faith in the "good tsar." Soon after, the country was gripped by waves of workers' strikes. The strikers formed their councils, or soviets, which began to wield political power in the towns affected by the movement. In June, there was a mutiny in the Black Sea on the armored cruiser *Potemkin*, which two decades later became the subject of a famous silent film by Sergei Eisenstein. By October 1905, Russia was paralyzed by a general strike.

This was a turning point. Prime Minister Sergei Witte presented the emperor with a stark choice: a constitution or a bloodbath. On October 17, 1905, Nicholas II issued a manifesto in which he granted his subjects certain personal, civil, and political rights, and established a State Duma as a form of parliament. The manifesto fell short of a constitution, but for the first time in Russian history it led to the sharing of power between the tsar and the people. Russia's first revolution achieved a tangible result. Not everyone was satisfied – in December, Moscow witnessed an armed uprising – but things began to calm down. Elections to the Duma stimulated the creation of political parties. The liberal flank was led by the Constitutional Democrats; the center-right by the "Octoberists"; and the nationalist far right by the Union of Russian People. The left was represented by Labor, social democrats (radical Bolsheviks and moderate Mensheviks), and socialist revolutionaries.

Elections to the Duma in 1906, held on the basis of quotas for the main estates and professional and ethnic groups, returned a legislature highly critical of the government and, as it was unwilling to condemn revolutionary terror, it was dismissed. From 1907, the authorities went onto a counter-offensive. A new election law shifted the balance in favor of loyalist groups. New Prime Minister Pyotr Stolypin ruthlessly clamped down on terror. Courts-martial were installed, and hundreds of terrorists were executed. Order was re-established.

A conservative reformer, Stolypin sought political stability on the basis of the sanctity of private property. In his five years as prime minister, he managed to free peasants from the diktat of the community, and thus boosted market relations in agriculture. Peasants were now able to own land as individuals, not just to use it as members of the community. Stolypin's reforms also stimulated peasant migration from European Russia, where land was scarce, to the Far East. Within seven years, almost 4 million people crossed the Urals heading east.

Despite political turbulence, Russia's economy at the beginning of the twentieth century was developing more rapidly than that of any other major country. In 1914, the country's share of global GDP reached 7.4%, which placed it only behind the United States, Germany, and Great Britain.[5] In per capita terms, however, Russia lagged behind the developed nations; its labor productivity was but a fraction of that in Western Europe. Yet the country was clearly emerging as an economic powerhouse. Rapid population growth contributed to the belief that by the mid-twentieth century it would dominate Europe economically, politically, and militarily. This, however, was not to be. In 1914, the Russian Empire stumbled into a world war that physically destroyed it within less than three years.

World War I

Stolypin firmly stood for peace. This, however, was a difficult task in a Europe where tensions between opposing camps – the Anglo-French and the German-Austrian – were getting ever higher. Moreover, in 1911, Stolypin was assassinated by a terrorist-cum-police agent at a Kiev theater. (More than a century later, it is still not clear who might have been behind the attack.) The tsar was inclined, for ideological and family reasons, to improve relations with Germany, but Russia's financial dependence on France, with which St. Petersburg had also been in a formal alliance since 1891, also had to be taken into account. Russia tried hard to balance between the main rivals, but its historical involvement in the Balkans, for the sake of leading the Orthodox Slavic world and controlling the Turkish Straits, finally drew it into a confrontation with the central powers. On August 1, 1914, a month after the shots fired in Sarajevo, Germany declared war on Russia.

For some time before it went to war, Berlin had been developing ideas about world hegemony. A combination of German industrial power and Russia's vast resources and geopolitical reach would have made a Berlin-led alliance well-nigh invincible. Had it materialized, the fate of Europe and the world in the twentieth century would have been vastly different. Russia, however, was not willing to submit itself to Germany's tutelage. Instead, it threw in its lot with the

Western powers. Under those circumstances, German leaders decided to knock out France and hit Russia hard enough to make it sue for peace – which would be available on German terms. This did not work out as planned.

The beginning of the war was marked by a massive patriotic surge in Russia and its early tactical successes on the battlefield. These successes, however, were soon overturned. German forces routed the Russian armies in East Prussia. The Russian offensive, launched exactly as promised in the Russo-French war plan, made the Germans redeploy their troops from west to east, thus critically easing the pressure on the French and wrecking the Schlieffen Plan of the German General Staff, which foresaw capture of Paris during the initial stage of the war. The price that Russia had to pay for Paris's deliverance was 250,000 casualties.

In 1915, as Germany made defeating Russia its first priority, it managed to occupy Russia's Polish, Lithuanian, and western Belarusian provinces. The Russian army, particularly its officer corps, was decimated. Yet the Russians managed to stabilize the frontline, which would remain unchanged till the Bolshevik coup of 1917. In 1916, Russia staged a counter-offensive against the Austrians, and was advancing against the Turks in the south. As a precautionary measure, Russian forces also occupied northern Persia. By 1916, Russia's industry became adjusted to the war conditions, and by the spring of

1917, St. Petersburg was getting ready to launch a major counter-offensive.

Hoping for an eventual allied victory, Russian diplomats negotiated the war aims with their French and British allies, and got their assent for annexation of eastern Galicia and control over Constantinople and the Straits. Russia was also seeking Turkish Armenia and part of Kurdistan and the tsar was mulling over the possibility of restoring an independent Polish state in a personal union with Russia, on the Finnish model. None of this was realized – not so much because of the failure of the Russian army to defeat the enemy, but because of the failure of the tsar's government to keep order in the capital.

Domestic Crisis

The patriotic unity of the summer of 1914 soon gave way to old political divisions. Much of society had no trust in the authorities, and vice versa. Moreover, the purpose of the war that was proclaimed "Patriotic," on the model of the 1812 resistance to Napoleon, remained unclear to most ordinary people, including the private soldiers in the fighting army. Russians fight best when they fight in defense of their own country, or on some clear mission, such as liberation of Orthodox co-religionists or Slav co-ethnics from alien rule. By contrast, the war for Russia's great power interests in Europe, not unlike the one only a decade before for dominance in the Far East, was becoming widely resented. As during the 1905 revolution, an unpopular war eroded domestic support for the regime. In 1915, most members of the State Duma, which continued to function intermittently during the war, formed an opposition "Progressive Bloc" that demanded a representative government. Nicholas II rejected the demand, after which the stand-off between the tsarist authorities and the bulk of the political class went into the open.

By this point, the emperor had assumed the role of commander-in-chief and was spending much time at the front. As a result, he effectively entrusted the task of governing Russia to Empress Alexandra Feodorovna, who was heavily influenced by Grigori Rasputin. Rasputin, a former Siberian peasant-turned-healer, impressed Alexandra with his capacity to successfully treat her hemophiliac son and heir-to-the-throne, Alexei. This was as solid a foundation of Rasputin's position at the court as one could imagine. The imperial court, however, was fast becoming isolated within the country. Expectations of a new revolution were spreading.

Rasputin's antics and orgies were the talk of the capital, but his political influence was a much more serious matter. On his advice, prime ministers and other senior officials were changed frequently, and at will, often remaining in office only a few months. The pushback was forming. The Western allies hated Rasputin, who was against the war. Monarchists, in turn, saw him as a real threat to the legitimacy of the monarchy. In December 1916, they killed him. It very soon became clear, however, that even with the removal of Rasputin, the threat remained. Rasputin himself had prophesied that his assassination would usher in a catastrophe and that the emperor would be overthrown within six months after his own death. This is precisely what happened.

Bolshevik leader Vladimir Ulyanov, known as Lenin, sitting in his Swiss exile and urging his supporters to work toward Russia's defeat, so that the "world imperialist war" could be turned into a "world proletarian revolution," had no clue how close the revolution was in Russia. In January 1917, he opined that his generation of radicals would not see it.[6] The following month, the Russian monarchy was toppled. The issue was not the economy. It was politics.

Revolution Strikes Again

During the war, Russia's agriculture did not suffer too much. Russia was the only European nation at war which did not need to introduce food rationing. As always, Russian resources seemed limitless. Yet, as people were getting war-weary, and daily difficulties were mounting, chance played its fateful role. Shortage of bread in Petrograd, as St. Petersburg was renamed after the outbreak of the war, led to panic, women's demonstrations, and workers' strikes that paralyzed the city. Soldiers refused to carry out orders to crush the protests and joined with the protesters.

On February 28, 1917, workers and rebel soldiers took over the capital and arrested the government. The Petrograd Soviet proclaimed "democratization of the army," which allowed soldiers not to follow orders. This order delivered a deadly blow against one of the principal pillars of the Russian state. The army, which traditionally protected the country from its external enemies, and was frequently used to keep order inside, started to disintegrate. Instead of moving to put down the revolt, which would have resulted in numerous casualties but would probably have restored order and saved the country, on March 2 Nicholas II chose to abdicate for himself and his son. He offered the crown to his younger brother, Grand Duke Mikhail, who promptly refused it. Russia's millennium-long monarchy was gone.

The Russian Empire was by no means doomed to end the way it did, but nor was its demise totally fortuitous. The 1905 revolution had laid bare Russia's many domestic conflicts, most of which remained unresolved. The new revolution, like its predecessor, was provoked by an unpopular and unsuccessful war. However, it could only triumph because the political regime, and the person embodying it, lost the respect of the subjects, and ultimately lost control of the situation. That sealed the country's fate.

The Provisional Government

Between March and October 1917, Russia was ruled by a Provisional Government, which was formed by members of the Duma. The new government's main task was to lead the way to a Constituent Assembly which would determine Russia's new political order. The legitimacy of the new authorities, however, was questionable, as was their ability to govern. The Provisional Government, which was headed by a coalition of liberal and center-right parties, proved absolutely unable to put down the anarchy that was fast spreading in the country. After the monarchy, the Russian state itself was fast going down.

The government also had a powerful rival, the Petrograd Soviet, led by moderate socialists. Whereas the government had its roots in the Duma, the Soviet had the street on its side. The Soviet did not so much try to unseat the government as constantly pressured it "in the name of the revolution." It also created a parallel nationwide system of governance in the form of local soviets. The soviets advertised themselves as "workers' and soldiers' committees" opposed to the "bourgeois" government and the former tsarist administration. To a superficial observer, revolutionary Russia demonstrated "duality of power." In reality, anarchy increasingly prevailed throughout the country.

The euphoria of freedom did not last long. The revolution let loose the long-pent-up energies of the common people, which the government was unable to curb and the soviets tried to exploit. Neither the liberals nor the center-right politicians or even the moderate socialists could do much about it. It was at this moment that a minor radical socialist group, the Bolsheviks, numbering just 5,000 members in February 1917, stepped forward. In April 1917, their leader, Lenin, returned to Russia from Swiss exile, traveling across Germany in a sealed railroad car provided by the German General Staff, who funded the Bolsheviks, hoping to knock Russia out of the war. Upon arrival in Petrograd, Lenin immediately proclaimed his program: "no support for the Provisional Government"; "all power to the soviets"; "immediate peace without annexations and indemnities"; "land to the peasants"; and "factories to the workers."[7]

Lenin did not care about his critics, who were many; he appealed to the gut feelings of the masses, who increasingly supported his program. The party membership grew; crucially, it managed to create its own military force, the Red Guards. In May 1917, Lenin was joined in Petrograd by Lev Trotsky, the theorist of a "permanent revolution," who had returned from American exile. Lenin was a political genius; Trotsky, a genius of organization. Together, they formed a powerful winning team. In June, Lenin declared that his party, which now included the Trotskyites, was ready to take all power in the land. His first attempt to stage a coup, in July, ended in failure. Lenin had to flee to

Finland, still part of Russia but out of bounds to the Russian police.

The Provisional Government reconstituted itself. The new prime minister and war minister was Alexander Kerensky, a socialist whose political allies dominated the new government. Kerensky was widely popular among the educated classes, but he found governing extremely difficult. Russia's economic and financial situation was becoming dire. The war, which the government continued to wage out of solidarity with the allies, was bringing new losses, but no victory. Fearful of unfavorable results, the Provisional Government was putting off elections to the Constituent Assembly. It was clear that Kerensky was unable to prevent the coming catastrophe.

As an eleventh-hour move, in late August 1917, General Lavr Kornilov, the new commander-in-chief, insisted on the need for strong leadership to save the country. Kerensky managed to outflank Kornilov and present him as a would-be usurper and "butcher of the revolution." The government was more concerned with a possible restoration of the monarchy than a radical socialist coup. To forestall such a restoration, without waiting for the Constituent Assembly elections, Russia was proclaimed a republic. Kerensky, however, underestimated Lenin and his followers. Less than two months after the end of the "Kornilov mutiny," the Bolsheviks seized power and established a regime that ruled the country for the next three-quarters of a century. Crucial to the Bolsheviks' victory was their success in revolutionizing the 10 million-strong Russian army, whose private soldiers not only refused to obey officers, but also deserted en masse and headed back to their villages.

Bolshevik Takeover

For weeks, Lenin, with his superb political instincts, had been urging his followers to topple the Provisional Government, against the opinion of those who preferred to wait for an all-Russian Congress of the soviets.[8] On October 24, 1917, the coup mechanism was set in motion. On the following day, Kerensky fled Petrograd for the front, and the Bolshevik Red Guards, in a virtually bloodless move, took over the critical points in the city, including the Winter Palace, and arrested the government. On October 26, Lenin proclaimed the victory of a "workers' and peasants' revolution." Like the tsarist authorities in February, its successor government ceded power within three days. Russia entered a completely new period in its history, though very few people understood it at the time.

The first decrees of the Bolshevik government – the Council of People's Commissars, as it called itself – dealt with the issues of peace and land. Lenin called on the warring nations to immediately cease hostilities and begin talks about "democratic peace." To Russia's peasants, he offered "socialization" of the land and restoration of the community. The new government was formally established by a Congress of the

Soviets, and was to stay in power till the Constituent Assembly, which was due to convene in January 1918. Lenin, Trotsky, and their associates, however, had no intention to hand over power. They did not see themselves as another provisional government, but rather as a full-fledged dictatorship, in the name of the workers, the "proletariat."

Lenin, who was very much a practical man as well as a theorist and a politician, lost no time. The decree on the press, passed just two days after the takeover, banned all "counter-revolutionary" publications. The government, still formally responsible to the soviets, wrested the right to issue decrees without the approval of the soviets' central committee. The Bolsheviks took control of the state's financial resources. The decree on courts abolished written law and replaced it with "revolutionary consciousness." Enterprises were placed under workers' control, and then nationalized. The fighting army was placed under Bolshevik control, and partially demobilized. Repression followed. Political parties that did not recognize Bolshevik rule were outlawed, and their leaders arrested, some summarily killed. In December 1917, an "extraordinary commission" was founded to "fight against counter-revolution and sabotage" – the future feared secret police. Within six months, Bolshevik rule – "soviet power" as it was called – was established across most of Russia. With some exceptions, notably in Moscow, there was no resistance.

Bolshevik leaders were brilliant tacticians, but also

doctrinaire ideologues, radical followers of Karl Marx
and Friedrich Engels. The *Communist Manifesto* and
Das Kapital were their guiding lights. They saw the revolution in Russia as little more than a match to light the
fire of a world revolution that would end capitalism,
abolish private property alongside the oppressive state,
and establish a society of abundance based on socialist
and communist principles. Their main hope was for
an early revolution in Germany and other advanced
countries in Europe. It would be victorious European
socialism that would lead the way for more backward
countries, such as Russia. Before that happened, however, the Bolsheviks went on demolishing Russia's old
regime, along with its laws, morals, and religion.

Peace with Germany; Break-Up of the Empire

Elections to the Constituent Assembly which were
held in the fall of 1917 gave the Bolsheviks less than
a quarter of the vote; socialist revolutionaries, popular among the peasants, polled nearly 40%, and
almost 60% with their Ukrainian and Muslim allies;
by contrast, liberals got just 5%; the right-wing parties, 3%; and the Mensheviks, under 3%.[9] Denied a
majority, the Bolsheviks saw the assembly as a threat.
They allowed it to open in January 1918, only to
dismiss it with the force of arms the following day
after it had refused to ratify their decrees. In its place,
the Bolsheviks promptly convened the Congress of
Soviets that they controlled, which proclaimed Russia

a Soviet Federative Socialist Republic (RSFSR). In July 1918, the first Soviet constitution was adopted.

While Lenin's decree on peace had no effect on the warring parties, the Bolshevik government in November 1917 opened separate peace talks with the German military command. Initially the idea was to bid for time until a revolution in Germany, which the Bolsheviks saw as imminent. The revolution, however, was not forthcoming, and the Germans were pressing the Bolsheviks hard, demanding major territorial concessions as a price for peace. The Bolshevik leadership was split. First, Trotsky, the commissar for foreign affairs, won support for his "no war, no peace, and sending the army home" formula, seeking to provoke a German offensive which, in his calculation, would lead to a workers' revolution in Europe. The Germans did resume their offensive, but the European workers remained in place. Then, *in extremis*, Lenin prevailed in imposing the terms of peace on his colleagues, in order to save the Soviet Russian regime. Lenin the proletarian revolutionary was thus turning into a Soviet Russian statesman.

The peace treaty was signed on March 3, 1918, in Brest-Litovsk. It was exceedingly harsh. Russia lost Poland, Ukraine, the Baltic provinces, and part of Belarus with 56 million people – about a third of its population. In addition, Russia was to pay Germany a heavy financial "compensation." In return, the Bolsheviks got diplomatic recognition from Russia's principal western neighbor. While Germany was busy redeploying its forces for the last offensive on the western front, the Bolsheviks got a breathing space to consolidate their hold on power within Russia. When in November 1918 exhausted Germany signed an armistice with the Entente powers and at last plunged into a revolution of its own, the Soviet government annulled the Brest-Litovsk treaty.

By that time, however, the Russian Empire was no more. Already in December 1917, Lenin agreed to Finland's independence; Poland, under German occupation since 1915, was being restored as a result of the Entente victory; Lithuania, Latvia, and Estonia proclaimed their sovereignty; Ukraine signed its own peace with Germany as an independent state; and Bessarabia was occupied, and then annexed, by Romania. These developments were followed in May 1918 by the independence of Georgia, Azerbaijan, and Armenia. The Bolsheviks held on to Turkestan, but within Russia proper their position was far from stable. After a period of shock, resistance to the new regime was emerging in several places. A civil war in Russia was about to begin.

Civil War

Fighting was sparked off in May 1918 by the Czechoslovak corps, composed of former Austro-Hungarian POWs en route to the western front. Bolshevik rule was toppled in a number of major cities along the railroad the corps was traveling by

– from the Volga region to Siberia. In Moscow itself, which from March 1918 again became the capital of Russia, left-wing social revolutionaries, who formed a government coalition with the Bolsheviks, rebelled. At the same time, a group of social revolutionaries took control of Yaroslavl, a city north of Moscow. The Bolsheviks, having put down the revolts that threatened their own headquarters, decided to take no chances. In July, former emperor Nicholas II, his wife and five children, and their servants, who had been under arrest since March 1917, were killed in Ekaterinburg in the Urals, almost certainly on orders from Moscow. A number of other members of the imperial family were killed in the summer of 1918.

In late August 1918, Lenin himself was shot and wounded. The Bolsheviks formally announced "Red Terror." Their aim was physical extermination of the former Russian ruling class as such. Apart from the "bourgeoisie," the "hostile elements" included intelligentsia, the clergy, Cossacks, and other groups. The Russian Orthodox Church, which in 1917 was liberated from the bureaucratic control of the tsar, was practically declared an enemy of the state by the atheist Bolshevik authorities. Through to the end of the Civil War, the number of those killed by the "Reds" is estimated to have been between 500,000 and 2 million people. From the summer of 1918, a system of concentration camps was organized.

The anti-Bolshevik forces, collectively called the "Whites," ranged from monarchists and nationalists to liberals and socialists of all stripes. They never managed to unite, but they mounted several military campaigns. Many Russians refused to accept Bolshevism hands down. The "White Movement" began already in November 1917 in the Don region in southern Russia, where Generals Alexeyev and Kornilov and Cossack atamans Kaledin and Krasnov organized a Volunteer Army. Under the command of General Denikin, the Whites came within 250 kilometers of Moscow. In Siberia, Admiral Kolchak was proclaimed the supreme ruler of all Russia, and was threatening "red" Moscow from the east. In the northwest, Generals Yudenich and Miller advanced on the outskirts of Petrograd. All these efforts, however, were essentially uncoordinated, and the White forces were relatively small compared to their enemies.

The "Workers' and Peasants' Red Army" was largely the creation of Trotsky, now the people's commissar for war. In July 1918, universal conscription was introduced, and the Bolshevik-held territories began to be turned into a single military camp. Within a year, owing to mass mobilization, the Red Army's strength reached 3 million. The young peasants and workers in its ranks were professionally trained and led: most of the commanders were former tsarist officers and generals. These "military specialists," as they were called, were under close observation and control by the commissars placed at their side by the Communist Party. The motives of the 50,000 officers of the old regime who were mobilized or chose to serve the Bolsheviks varied: some sympathized with the Communist cause; others faced uncertain, and likely dire, consequences if they refused mobilization orders; still others saw the Bolsheviks as the probable winners, the new state, and were ready to serve Russia again – even under their rule. The dilemmas of the Russian officer corps were vividly depicted by Mikhail Bulgakov in his novel *The White Guard* (1925) and the play *The Days of the Turbins* (1926).

Eventually, the Reds managed to defeat their opponents. In November 1920, Crimea, the last major foothold of the White armies, fell to the Reds. General Pyotr Wrangel sailed for Constantinople with 150,000 troops. In 1921, the Soviet forces occupied the South Caucasus. By 1922, the bulk of the former imperial territory was under the control of the Bolsheviks. Only Finland, Poland, and the Baltic provinces managed to stay independent, and Bessarabia was incorporated into Romania. Foreign forces – American, British, Czechoslovak, French, German, Japanese, Polish, and Turkish troops, who intervened in various parts of Russia, from Archangel and Murmansk in the north to Odessa and Baku in the south, and from Kiev in the west to Vladivostok in the east – had all departed, leaving the Bolsheviks in control.

Western Intervention

Major Western powers – Britain, France, and the United States – did not recognize the Bolshevik regime until many years after the October 1917 revolution. Neither did they engage decisively to strangle it in its cradle. They sent troop contingents to Russia, and gave some material support to the Whites, but they were wary of the revolutionary contagion which might have been caught by their own lower classes, including their members in uniform. They were also careful not to become too involved in Russian domestic affairs, in part out of fear of helping restore a powerful competitor. Their de facto policy was to keep Russia in limbo, weakening it geopolitically and isolating its extremist regime. Russia was not invited to attend the 1919 Versailles peace conference and the League of Nations, on the plausible grounds of there being no recognized Russian government in place, but tellingly no place was reserved in the new international institutions for Russia, which had been a major ally till 1917.

Reflecting on this later, thoughtful Russians realized that their country simply could not rely on the West – it would not help them in their hour of need and would seek to further weaken them when it found itself in dire straits. All the sacrifices that Russia brought to the altar of allied victory were lost, and essentially not recognized. The Versailles system went on to function not only without Germany, the defeated enemy, but also without Russia, the nominal ally. The system, as it turned out, was doomed from the start.

Reasons for the Red Victory

There were a number of reasons for the Reds' victory, but two were really crucial. The first was that most peasants – who formed the bulk of the population – saw the Whites as agents of restoration of the old regime, and the White Terror, even though it was generally a pale version of the Red one, did not help to win their hearts and minds. The Russian peasantry had no stake in the old Russian state. Lenin and the Bolsheviks managed to use the peasants' yearning to be masters of their land, and their communal instinct, to the advantage of the Communist system.

The other main reason was the insistence of the White leaders on a "unified and indivisible Russia," which threatened to take away the newly won administrative and cultural autonomy of dozens of Russia's ethnic groups. In the end, the Bolsheviks, who fought the war under the slogan of national self-determination, managed to consolidate the former empire, albeit in a novel and very different form, whereas the Whites, who hoped to restore the old empire, ended up as émigrés. About a million Russians left their country fleeing the Bolsheviks. Most of them settled in France, Germany, Czechoslovakia, Yugoslavia, and China. From now on, Russia fully belonged to Lenin and his followers, who, in spite of their ideological fervor and revolutionary internationalism, managed to hold power in a country far from ideal for their social experiment and proved themselves capable not only of demolishing the old regime, but of building a wholly new state in its place.

From Tsarism to Communism

Responsibility is one of the key themes that stands out from the first two decades of Russia's twentieth-century history. A Russian autocrat is a person with enormous power. However, that person is also saddled with a most heavy responsibility. Nicholas II was not doomed to end up in the cellar of a house in Ekaterinburg where he was murdered alongside his family. His stubborn insistence on the inviolability of absolutist power; his lack of interest in state affairs and a clear preference for his family; and the weakness of his character all turned out to be fatal flaws. A family man like him would be a model; a monarch like him could have survived in calmer times, even in Russia. Nicholas's tragedy was that he turned out woefully unequal to the task of a Russian ruler in the times of upheaval.

The opponents of the tsarist regime – from liberals to social revolutionaries – bear a responsibility of their own. They focused on demolishing what they hated, rather than on constructing what they aspired to be an alternative. They also fancied themselves representatives of the people, whom they barely knew, looked down upon, and often misunderstood. They sought to topple the regime – and destroyed the state; they proclaimed democracy, which immediately turned into a chaos that they did not control; and they failed to manage their own differences – falling an easy prey to the ruthless group that established a totalitarian regime in place of tsarist authoritarianism.

Next to the politicians' responsibility, the state of society's morals was crucial. In the early twentieth century, Russian society at large was going through a comprehensive crisis, and the 1905 and 1917 revolutions richly testify to that. Traditional values were losing their hold on many people, and religious faith became much weaker. The central pillars of Russian social life, God, the tsar, and the fatherland, gave way at the same time. Revolutions and wars destroyed the popular belief in the sanctity of life and much devalued it. Russia's cultural figures lost the holistic view that marked their nineteenth-century predecessors; their worldview became fragmented. The great upheaval changed the Russian people for ever.

The fall of the monarchy in February 1917 was celebrated by Russian liberals and many in the West as opening a chance for Russia to become a liberal democracy – a chance that, eight months later, was nipped in the bud by the Bolsheviks. Tellingly, a similar attitude showed itself toward the end of the twentieth century when the fall of the Communist regime seemed to open another opportunity for the Russian people to embrace a Western-style political system – an opportunity that was taken away by a former KGB officer-turned-president, Vladimir Putin. In both cases, domestic liberals and their Western well-wishers ignored the fact that periods of nominal democracy in Russia – whether in 1917 or in the 1990s – were marked by the de facto self-destruction of the state, with disastrous consequences for most ordinary people.

Like three centuries before, during the Time of Troubles, Russia almost ceased to exist. The country's old system and the people's way of life were destroyed more thoroughly than ever before. Millions of people died, while those who survived went on to construct a society that had never existed in history. Within years, Russia re-emerged as a country, state, and society even more consolidated – often forcefully – than before. Having been excluded from the international system as a result of its own revolutionary experiment and "sanitary" containment from the outside, Russia was soon poised to make a stunning comeback.

2

The Rise of the Soviet State (1921–38)

Having won the domestic Civil War, but at the same time having been disappointed over the failure of workers' revolutions in Germany and elsewhere in Europe, Russian Bolsheviks had to make the switch from wartime practices and revolutionary ambitions to the daily routine of political, economic, and social transformation of the vast but essentially isolated country that they now controlled. Russia was no longer the match to light a global rebellion against capitalism, only to be guided and assisted later by the victorious revolutionary brethren from the advanced West. It now had to implement the Marxist utopia on its own, encircled by class enemies.

Socialism in One Country

The experiment that was socialism in one country was absolutely unprecedented, breathtaking, and stunning. Essentially, the Bolsheviks set out to create a wholly new world: a new non-capitalist economy, a new classless internationalist society, a new atheist consciousness, and a new man. They saw their exercise in world-historical terms, not as a national endeavor. Although Russia had not sparked a world revolution, it was turning into an example for the rest of the world to follow – in the quest for a new humanity. All inherited conventions and old limitations were thrown out, including moral ones. Russian Communists were, as a popular phrase went, doing nothing less than "storming the sky."

But they were also careful to look under their feet. Lenin's political genius lay in his uncanny ability to adapt to fast-changing circumstances. Unlike Marxism, which was a critique of capitalism that had little to say about the post-capitalist future, Leninism was essentially a practical guide to achieving specific objectives. Lenin built a militant party, a political war machine; seized power in a vast land; ruthlessly eliminated the old regime along with its supporters; cowed or cajoled a huge population; and prevailed in a bloody civil war. He always did what seemed to him to be the right thing at any given moment, pressuring his slower-thinking allies and reversing himself when necessary. With the revolution completed and the Civil War won, Lenin's task was to make sure that the new regime would survive under less violent conditions.

Leninism was almost all about politics, but once peace broke out in Russia, the most urgent task was economic. During the Civil War, the Bolsheviks practiced "war communism," a money-free system of forcible confiscation of agricultural produce for subsequent distribution according to the revolutionary state's needs. By the end of the war, this system became untenable. Numerous peasant uprisings and a military mutiny threatened Bolshevik rule. Severe famine broke out in the Volga provinces. Lenin promptly changed course and implemented what was dubbed the New Economic Policy (NEP). To many of both his followers and his adversaries this looked like a complete reversal. In 1921, confiscation of peasants' produce was replaced by taxation. Market relations were again allowed so that the peasants could freely sell fruits of their labor. A currency reform replaced essentially worthless Soviet paper notes with real money backed by gold.

Lenin's goal was not so much to give respite to the war-weary population as to shore up the political system. This system was officially called Soviet, but in reality this was a Communist Party dictatorship disguised as working-class rule. The official name of the state was part of an exercise in political window-dressing. The soviets – from local councils to the All-Russian Congress of Soviets and its, in theory, all-powerful Executive Committee – were a superficial decoration. The actual rulers of the land sat on the Central Committee of the Communist Party and controlled its increasingly powerful apparatus. The Central Committee appointed party members to serve as chairmen and secretaries of the soviets at different levels and essentially dictated policy to them.

Having won the Civil War and embarked on socialist transformation, the Bolsheviks did not stop fighting against political enemies, real or imagined, and

would-be opponents. They believed that their enemies would never accept defeat. The apparatus of
the secret political police, initially nicknamed the
Chekah, now officially called the OGPU, expanded
greatly and covered the entire country. During
the 1920s, 600,000 people were condemned for
"counter-revolutionary crimes." From 1928, a long
series of public trials started to terrorize the country.
By 1930, the newly created administration of concentration camps, the so-called GULAG, housed 150,000
prisoners. Solovki, an island monastery in the White
Sea that was turned into a huge prison, became an
early symbol of growing repression. Creating a new
humanity, it seemed, meant eliminating many of those
who did not or would not fit in.[1]

The Founding of the Soviet Union

The triumphant Communist Party also set about con-
solidating its rule across much of the territory of the
former Russian Empire. By 1922, there existed four
nominally independent Soviet republics: the Russian
Federation (which at that time also included Central
Asia), Ukraine, Belarus, and the Transcaucasus
Federation of Armenia, Azerbaijan, and Georgia.
In reality, however, the ruling Communist parties
of Ukraine, Belarus, and Transcaucasus were but
branches of the Russian Communist Party. During the
Civil War, the Communist-dominated entities formed
a military, diplomatic, and financial union. Now the

time had come to unify them in a single state. The issue was what kind of a state: a unitary or a federal one?

Lenin, Trotsky, and their closest followers were self-avowed internationalists. What mattered to them were class distinctions, rather than ethnicity or nationality. They reviled the imperial Russian state, calling it "a prison for nations." Lenin, ever-pragmatic and dialectical, however, backed national self-determination to nip nationalism in the bud. His logic was simple: class origins and economic factors – the only ones that really counted, in his Marxist view – would bind workers of different nationalities together. "Workers of the world" belonged to no particular country or nation, unlike the "bourgeoisie," which had national roots. Borders among countries where revolution has triumphed might stay, although they would be meaningless. And, in a paradoxical twist, it was reasoned that if everyone had the right to be separate, then no one would want to do so. In a nutshell, Lenin was a Communist federalist.

Josef Stalin, then the party's main expert on nationalities, was less sanguine. Hailing from Georgia, he knew more about national feelings and sensitivities. He preferred not to take chances and urged the inclusion of the three non-Russian republics into Soviet Russia as autonomous units, denying them the right to secede. Lenin strongly disagreed with this "unitarist" view and had his way. The Union of Soviet Socialist Republics (USSR), which was proclaimed at the Bolshoi Theater on December 30, 1922, was based on the formal right of each constituent republic to secede. Crucially, however, there was a single dominant party throughout the union that would effectively prevent separatism – if need be, by force. Thus, Lenin won on the form, while Stalin's view prevailed on the substance.

To make the union meaningful, and win the support of the dozens of ethnic groups making up the new USSR, the central authorities began to extend generous economic subsidies to the borderlands; they supported and promoted ethnic languages; they fostered an ethnic intelligentsia, provided, of course, that its members were loyal to the new regime; and they created academies of sciences in each republic, founded universities, built theaters, and the like, in order to create positive stimuli for non-Russian groups to stick to the union. Indeed, it was "Great-Russian chauvinism," rather than "bourgeois nationalism," that was the main worry for Lenin and his supporters.

The "flowering of ethnic cultures" had one important caveat, though: everyone in the USSR was subjected to strict ideological and political control. As the phrase went, various nationalities' cultures could be ethnic in form, but had to be socialist in content. The Bolsheviks' ambitions went beyond the former Russian Empire. The Soviet Union adopted the red banner as its flag; the hammer and sickle emblazoned on the globe as its official emblem; and the *Internationale* as its anthem. The name of Russia, associated with the ancient regime, was de-emphasized and replaced by the word "Soviet." Three-quarters of a century later, when the rule of the Communist Party weakened, the right to secession contained in all Soviet constitutions doomed the Soviet Union, but it also allowed its relatively orderly dismantlement.

Struggle for Power: Stalin Wins

Lenin's intervention on the founding principle of the USSR was one of his last political acts. From 1923, his health was rapidly deteriorating, and in January 1924 he died aged 53. Lenin was the first Russian leader with a truly global and lasting impact, but far less as a Russian statesman than as a Communist revolutionary. He managed to turn the teaching of a German economist into a world-transformative idea. Much of the twentieth century was driven by Leninist ideas, parties, and guiding principles.

Lenin's death ushered in the Soviet Union's first succession crisis. By the time of his passing, the struggle for power within the Bolshevik leadership had already started. To most outsiders, Trotsky, the actual leader of the coup in Petrograd in October 1917, the founder of the Red Army, a leading theorist and a powerful orator, was the obvious candidate. Stalin, however, was resolved to ruin Trotsky's ambitions. Long underestimated as a "gray mediocrity," he took control of the party's apparatus as its general secretary, then a purely technical position, and struck tactical alliances with other Bolshevik leaders who feared Trotsky: Grigory Zinoviev and Lev Kamenev. With the party's unity officially regarded as sacred, and public politics non-existent, Stalin's intrigues defeated Trotsky's charisma. The loser was first banished to Soviet Central Asia and then exiled to Turkey. With Trotsky out of the way, Stalin then outmaneuvered his occasional allies and by 1927 became the clear *primus inter pares* in the Politburo, the party's top ruling body.

The Stalin–Trotsky battle was not only about personal ambitions; it also had ideological and political dimensions. Trotsky continued to believe in a "permanent revolution" that would "sweep away world capitalism." Stalin, in contrast, focused on building socialism here and now. Although not discarding wholly the idea of a world revolution, he would bide his time until "imperialist contradictions" would again lead to turmoil and create openings – not so much for local Communists as for the Soviet Union. Eventually, in 1940, Trotsky was assassinated in Mexico by one of Stalin's agents. Although a victim of Stalin's terror, Trotsky was hardly a better alternative to Stalin. He cared as little about the lives of other humans and till his last days was working to foment a world revolution. A global revolutionary fire was his life's dream.

With Stalin in the driver's seat, it was the party's personnel policy that became the key instrument of political control. As head of the apparatus, Stalin personally managed the party's *nomenklatura*: some 4,000 key positions in the country to which he appointed his candidates. By 1929, when he turned 50, Stalin was no longer just a first among equals; he assumed absolute power in the land. His own cult of personality became a major tool of transforming not just the political environment and the ideological landscape in the country, but the country's very identity. It was no longer the ideals of the revolution, or the teachings of Lenin, Marx, and Engels, that mattered, but Stalin's personal attitude and his word. As Lenin was posthumously elevated to an icon, the Soviet Union began to live in the name of Stalin.

The Great Terror

Establishing a personal dictatorship was not enough for Stalin. He proceeded to replace the entire ruling Communist elite, some of whose members, although demoted and weakened, either still considered themselves his equals, or bore grudges against him. The murder in 1934 of Sergei Kirov, the party secretary in Leningrad (as St. Petersburg/Petrograd was renamed after Lenin's death), who was becoming more popular within the party *nomenklatura* than Stalin, provided a useful pretext. In all probability, the assassination was a common crime, but Stalin accused his rivals of being behind it. In the wave of Great Terror that followed in 1936–8, there were executions of party notables such as Zinoviev and Kamenev; the top ideologue Nikolai Bukharin; Alexei Rykov, Lenin's successor as head of the Soviet government; along with three of the five marshals of the Soviet Union, including the brilliant and ambitious Mikhail Tukhachevsky. A great many ordinary people suffered too. Of the 1.5 million arrested at the time, almost 700,000 were killed.[2] In place of the Bolshevik old guard, Stalin appointed people mostly of working-class background with little education, but much energy, and absolute personal loyalty to himself.

In 1936, amid the repression, Stalin promulgated a new Soviet constitution. It was based on the notions of socialism in one country and a classless society. The constitution supposedly guaranteed civil and political rights and freedoms to all people, including democratic elections. The caveat was that those rights had to be exercised "in the interests of the working people," that is, in a manner decided by the Communist Party. The constitution also proclaimed social rights – to work, to rest, to free education, health care, and so on. It established a new generally elected parliament, the Supreme Soviet, which would, however, meet only a few days per year. The Supreme Soviet's presidium, a permanent body, would function as a token collective presidency of the USSR. Of course, real power in the Soviet Union continued to belong to the Communist Party Central Committee, its apparatus, and the ruling Politburo, but essentially to Stalin himself, who earned a new nickname within the *nomenklatura*: "the Master."

Industrialization

In the economic arena, following Lenin's 1921 turn toward the market with the NEP, a hybrid system emerged. The market existed side by side with firm state control of the "commanding heights" of the economy. This maneuver brought immediate relief. In 1924, the Soviet budget rose to about half of the imperial one a decade before. By 1928, agricultural and industrial production reached their 1913 levels. Proper legal codes were introduced to replace arbitrary "revolutionary consciousness." Such a dramatic retreat from Communist principles raised fears among many Bolsheviks of a "sellout to the bourgeoisie," even as it instilled hopes in others of a gradual "normalization" of the regime. In fact, the NEP represented neither. This was a tactical step designed to consolidate political power through economic concessions. Already in 1928, Stalin proclaimed that the NEP had exhausted itself. He then proceeded to build a socialist economy.

Stalin's main goal was to quickly build a solid industrial base to arm and equip a strong military. Like virtually all senior Bolsheviks, he believed that war against "Western imperialists" was inevitable. "We are lagging behind them by 50–100 years," he declared; "unless we close that gap in 10 years, we'll be crushed."[3] The emphasis was logically placed on heavy industry, mainly coal and steel production. In 1928, the first five-year plan of economic development was launched. Almost immediately, the country turned into a huge building site. In the dozen years before World War II broke out, heavy industry expanded between 400 and 500%, with new branches of production – such as tractor, airplane, and automobile plants – springing up. Defense production – particularly of tanks, airplanes, and artillery pieces – increased between 1,200 and 1,800%. In anticipation of a war in the west, new industrial bases were built in Siberia. There and elsewhere, new towns and cities were founded. By contrast, consumer goods production was growing only slowly: private consumption in the Soviet Union in the 1930s was 15% lower than in 1913. Still, even by very conservative estimates, the Soviet economy in 1928–40 grew by 6% annually.[4]

In terms of organization, this was less of a planned economy than a command one. Political necessity was everything. Commands from Moscow were orders. The State Planning Committee (Gosplan) ruled supreme on behalf of the party. The volume of production was the main criterion. Money played only an auxiliary role, and profit was irrelevant. Management was centralized. Dozens of ministries were created, each responsible for a branch or sector of the economy. Foreign trade, monopolized by the state immediately after the revolution, was minimal. Preparing for a war with the capitalist world, which he considered inevitable, Stalin banked on autarky. Of course, the Soviet Union needed foreign technology and machine tools, which it bought mostly in Europe, chiefly Germany, and in the United States. The Great Depression made this easier and cheaper. To the world, however, rapid Soviet industrialization contrasted sharply with the economic crisis engulfing Europe and America.

Collectivization: the War on the Peasantry

Money for industrialization was to be provided by the countryside. In 1930, the Communist Party decided to "collectivize" agriculture, forcing individual peasants to join together and form collective farms. This move had more political than economic reasons behind it. Stalin regarded richer, usually more industrious and hard-working peasants – the "kulaks" (*fists*) – as class enemies and a breeding ground for "counter-revolution." They had to be removed from their local roots and sent into internal exile. By 1937, some 90% of the peasants were turned into "collective farmers," and 4 million "kulaks" were robbed of their property, deported from their native villages, and sent into the wilderness. About half of these people died. While Stalin and his associated were responsible for the general political decisions, identification of the targets and the individual fate of the victims was mostly decided by local party activists, neighbors motivated by greed or grudges, and so on.

Collectivization is often called a "second edition of serfdom." When in 1932 internal passports were first introduced in the Soviet Union, they were not issued to peasants. This made it impossible for them to travel outside of their village, change residence, take up work, or get any social service provided by the state, such as pensions. Collectivization immediately produced dire results: both yields and productivity fell. The peasants simply no longer had a stimulus to work. Not surprisingly, there was spontaneous push-back in a number of places against the government's policies. Bad harvests led the authorities to use terror against the peasants. The result was an artificially induced famine in 1932–3. It struck the main agricultural areas of the country: Ukraine, the Volga region, central Russia, the southern Urals, the Northern Caucasus, and Kazakhstan. The death toll was enormous: 6.5 million people died, 4 million of them in Ukraine alone.[5] This was a veritable war waged by the Communist leadership on the country's peasantry. The claim that *Holodomor* ("death by hunger") represented a genocide of the Ukrainian people is one of the founding tenets of the modern Ukrainian state. Its recognition by a number of parliaments and governments around the world reflects the political solidarity of most Western countries with Kiev.

Mass repression produced its own form of industrialization. From the 1930s to the early 1950s, the Soviet prison population at any one time averaged between 500,000 and 2.5 million.[6] The "camp industry" employed forced labor, essentially a form of slavery. GULAG labor built canals, railroads, and even cities, such as Norilsk. The writer Alexander Solzhenitsyn, who spent years in Stalin's jails, described the horrors of labor camps in *One Day in the Life of Ivan Denisovich* (1962), *In the First Circle* (1968), and then carefully chronicled it in *The Gulag Archipelago* (1973). Varlam Shalamov, Evgenia Ginzburg, and others also produced trenchant literary works about that incredibly tragic reality.[7]

Cultural Revolution and War on Religion

Communist leaders sought to breed a new kind of humans who would turn the Marxist utopia into Soviet, and then global, reality. They had to proceed from a low starting point. At the beginning, the key element in the Communist Party's social policy was combating illiteracy. They worked hard. Indeed, the literacy rate, which stood at 43% in 1920, jumped to 76% in 1938.[8] Teaching people to read and write was not an end in itself, of course. The party wanted to reach out to the common people with the printed word, and indoctrinate them with Communist ideology. State monopoly on all printed matter was established soon after the revolution. The Soviet school, after much revolutionary experimentation in the 1920s, was transformed into a traditional, fairly authoritarian institution dedicated to rote learning in social studies, while offering solid education in the sciences: precisely what the state needed. Industrialization required above all engineers and technicians, and technical colleges proliferated across the country.

The Bolsheviks initially vowed to revolutionize

culture. In reality the cultural level of the Russian people sank dramatically due to wars, revolutions, and the emigration of the educated classes, and there was an appalling decline in morality. With the period of turmoil over, the Communist Party resolved to bring more order and discipline to society. Women – those of the working class – were given voting rights and urged to break out of the kitchen and join social activities alongside men. Children's upbringing became a concern of the state. Young people's organizations were organized under Komsomol, a youth wing of the Communist Party. Children from 10 to 14 years old were drafted into the Young Pioneers, a scout-type organization, and primary school pupils were eligible to join the "Octoberists" – so named after the 1917 October revolution. Workers formed labor unions which were tightly run by the party. They cooperated with the management in enforcing very strict labor discipline, but also were responsible for sick leaves and vacations. The entire system was centralized and permeated by party propaganda.

Dissenting voices were silenced or exiled. In 1922, three "philosophers' steamships" took hundreds of leading members of the intelligentsia and their families to Germany. In retrospect, that exile, hard as it was, saved their lives. Many of those who stayed were jailed or executed. To take their place, new socialist intelligentsia would be "produced as in factories." An enormous effort was made to encourage young people to take up higher education. Dozens of new universities sprang up. The stress was laid on training technical engineers, mechanics, and specialists, as well as doctors and schoolteachers.

This policy of replacing old cadres with new ones greatly stimulated upward mobility in the country. Millions of members of formerly lower classes received a real chance to rise to important positions in virtually all walks of life, from science and technology to the medical profession to engineering. There was one major condition, however: they all had to stick to the ideological mainstream. The "correct political attitude" meant that ideology and the current needs of the party were more important that the facts. Those who expected to survive within the system had to acknowledge that and adapt.

The party paid special attention to forming the correct view of history. Seen from the Bolsheviks' very pragmatic angle, history was what they needed at any one time. The main interest, and thus prime emphasis, of course, was current history. Stalin himself took the trouble to heavily edit a *Short Course of the History of the All-Union Communist Party*, a volume published in 1938,[9] in which he laid down his interpretation of Russia's twentieth-century history, which would remain the official view, with some post-Stalin "corrections," through to the end of the Soviet Union.

Textbooks were not enough. The material environment was also changing. Some of the key cities got renamed: Petrograd became Leningrad; Tsaritsyn became Stalingrad; Perm changed its name to Molotov,

after Stalin's prime minister; Nizhny Novgorod,
was now known as Gorky, after the "great proletarian writer"; Tver became Kalinin, after the nominal
head of the Soviet state; and so on. Within all cities,
streets and squares altered their names, thousands
of churches were demolished, and countless monuments to Lenin, Stalin, Kirov, and other Bolshevik
leaders sprang up. When Lenin died, his body was
embalmed and kept on display in a mausoleum in
Moscow's Red Square, which became an obligatory
center of pilgrimage for ordinary Soviet people. In
the mid-1930s, central Moscow was redesigned, with
streets made much wider and a metro system, argua-
bly the best in the world, built. Stalin also made plans
for constructing huge public structures to totally alter
the capital's skyline, but the war intervened before
they were completed.

Early on, Lenin understood the importance of the
visual arts in a country with so many illiterate res-
idents. "Cinema," he said, was "the most important
art for us."[10] Films on the 1905 upheaval (*Battleship
Potemkin*, directed by Sergei Eisenstein, in 1925) and
the 1917 Bolshevik revolution (*Lenin in October* and
Lenin in 1918, directed by Mikhail Romm, in 1937
and 1939, respectively) became classics of Soviet film
art. The Ukrainian Alexander Dovzhenko was another
leading film director favored by Stalin. In literature, the
propaganda element was much less pronounced. The
poet Vladimir Mayakovsky's novel robust style symbolized the advent of a new era of post-revolutionary

construction, while Sergei Yesenin's lyrics provided a bridge to Russia's peasant tradition. In addition, *And Quiet Flows the Don* (1940), a major epic novel by the Nobel Prize winner Mikhail Sholokhov, delved incredibly deeply into the psyche of the Cossack society going through the revolutionary turmoil.

Soon, however, all art was placed under close politico-ideological supervision. Revolutionary avant-garde art was replaced by socialist realism. In 1934, in place of various associations, a single Writers' Union was formed, led by the renowned author Maxim Gorky. Other professional unions soon followed: of artists, composers, journalists, architects, and so on. Stalin, who closely oversaw the cultural scene, made sure that the Soviet people were gripped by genuine enthusiasm as trailblazers of a new progressive society, a model to the rest of the world. Grigory Alexandrov's film comedies featuring Lyubov Orlova, and Isaak Dunaevsky's rhythmic songs from the 1930s served that purpose much more effectively than sterile propaganda.

Artistic conformists were generously rewarded, while dissidents were expelled and essentially denied an ability to pursue a professional career. In the infamous words of Gorky, "If the enemy does not surrender, he will be annihilated."[11] Yet Russian literature did not die. The poets Anna Akhmatova and Boris Pasternak stayed in Russia and lived long enough to see the end of Stalin's rule. Osip Mandelstam died in prison in 1938. Mikhail Bulgakov died in his bed in

1940, but his life was made difficult. Marina Tsvetaeva, in desperation, committed suicide in 1941.

Bolshevism saw religion as its enemy, and even set a goal of destroying the church as an institution, and eliminating the very notion of God, by the twentieth anniversary of the revolution in 1937. Official atheism was wildly aggressive. In 1922–3, over 8,000 priests and monks were killed, over 600 monasteries closed, and the Patriarch Tikhon, elected in 1917 after a break of 200-plus years, was jailed. In 1931, Moscow's majestic Our Savior's cathedral was blown up. Yet during the 1937 census, 57% of respondents still called themselves believers. This realization of failure provoked more repression. In the three subsequent years, over 100,000 clergymen were killed. The number of churches was reduced from 25,000 in 1928 to just 1,300 in 1939. Of the 12,000 mosques, 10,000 were closed.[12]

From 1937, leaving the Soviet Union for anything other than official business was no longer allowed. The country was turning effectively into a besieged fortress. Proletarian internationalism was no longer sufficient. Soviet patriotism stepped forward to take its place, established on the firm foundation of the historical Russian state. The Russocentric worldview was making a comeback, as many alphabets of Turkic languages, originally switched from the Arabic to the Latin script, were now switched to Cyrillic. The recent dismissal of Russian pre-revolutionary history as uniformly bleak and oppressive was reversed. A case was being made for Russia's well-deserved leadership in the world revolutionary process. The centenary in 1937 of Alexander Pushkin's death was turned into a big event. Eisenstein was now directing films about medieval Russian figures, Prince Alexander Nevsky and Tsar Ivan the Terrible. Mikhail Glinka's nineteenth-century opera *Life for the Tsar* about the Russian people's resistance to Polish invaders during the Time of Troubles was again staged with great success, under the title *Ivan Susanin*, after its main hero. Tsarist-era military ranks were also restored.

Foreign Policy

Soviet foreign policy was another hybrid, like the economic policy of the 1920s, only longer-lasting. On one hand, Communists continued to work for a world revolution, even though it made them wait. On the other, having consolidated their control of a single major country, Russia, they had to practice "normal" diplomatic relations with the rest of the world, which remained under "bourgeois" control. Thus, the party's foreign policy had two arms. One was Comintern, the Communist International, in theory a unified world Communist Party, to which national parties, including the Russian one, belonged as national branches. In reality, Comintern was a department of the Russian (now officially called All-Union) Communist Party, which laid down its strategy and directed and financed its activities. That strategy, however, was essentially serving the interests of the Soviet state.

The other arm was the People's Commissariat for Foreign Affairs, or NKID in Russian. At the outset of the 1920s, Lenin the pragmatist formulated a concept of "peaceful coexistence" or "cohabitation" – a period of indefinite duration during which Soviet Russia would have to live side by side with capitalist countries: a major departure from Marxist doctrine. The Bolshevik "official" foreign policy was a paragon of pragmatism and *Realpolitik*. Already in 1918 in Brest-Litovsk, the Bolsheviks concluded a peace treaty, however unequal and hard for Russia, with Wilhelmine Germany, which saved their skin. In 1922, Russia and Germany, both excluded from the Versailles system, concluded another agreement at Rapallo. That opened the way to extensive economic and military cooperation between Moscow and Berlin. Russia sent agricultural produce to Germany, and imported industrial machinery; it also lent its territory to German military and industrial activity – involving tanks, airplanes, and chemical weapons – which was prohibited under the Versailles treaty.

Weimar Germany saw itself as a "central power" and pursued a see-saw foreign policy, or *Shaukelpolitik*. In the 1920s, Moscow did not regard Berlin as a military threat. Moreover, Georgi Chicherin, the commissar for foreign affairs from 1918 to 1930, developed a concept of uniting Europe's continental powers, first of all, Germany and France, against "British imperialism," which the Bolshevik leaders saw then as their main enemy. After the defeat of revolution in Europe, the thrust of the Comintern's efforts was directed at Asia, mainly British India and China. The Soviet Union also took care to stabilize relations with its immediate neighbors in Eastern Europe, as well as with Turkey, Iran, and Afghanistan. In 1924, the first-ever Labour government in Britain recognized the USSR. This was a turning point. In short order, most other leading countries followed suit, including France, Italy, Japan, and China. Only the United States stayed away, but economic relations with it flourished.

Hitler's coming to power in 1933 dramatically changed the situation for the USSR. Given the Nazis' anti-communist and racist views, Germany again came to be seen in the Kremlin as a source of war. Moscow changed course and started building coalitions against Hitler. In late 1933, US President Franklin D. Roosevelt moved to establish diplomatic relations with the Soviet Union. In 1934, the Soviet Union was invited to join the League of Nations. In 1935, the USSR concluded mutual assistance treaties with France and Czechoslovakia. On Stalin's orders, a Comintern congress urged European Communists to build anti-fascist "popular fronts" and help them to power. This strategy succeeded in France. In Spain, as a popular front government was attacked by the right-wing military, the Soviet Union intervened, sending arms shipments and 3,000 military advisers.

In the Far East, Moscow stopped attacking China's leader, Chiang Kai-shek, and formed an alliance with him against Japan. It dispatched 5,000 advisers to China, as well as 1,300 airplanes, 1,600 artillery pieces, and much other military equipment. Relations with Japan were getting tense, as Tokyo in 1936 entered the Anti-Comintern Pact with Germany. In 1938 and 1939, the Red Army clashed with Japan in brief border wars. In Europe, however, the Anglo-French policy of appeasing Nazi Germany, culminating in the 1938 Munich agreement to dismember Czechoslovakia, sent a chilling signal to Stalin that the Western powers were trying to pit Nazi Germany against the Soviet Union. He realized he would be left one-on-one with Hitler. Soviet foreign policy had to change again, and Maxim Litvinov, the people's commissar who succeeded Chicherin and was a proponent of cooperation with Britain and France, was dismissed in May 1939. Stalin put Vyacheslav Molotov, his former prime minister and a close aide, in his place. The outbreak of World War II was just months away.

Communist Transformation Completed

In the 17 years between the end of the Civil War in Russia and the outbreak of World War II, the Bolsheviks managed to build the foundation of the Soviet state that would last till the early 1990s. In that endeavor, the Communist Party could rely on the genuine enthusiasm of many ordinary people who believed they "were born to turn the fairy-tale into reality."[13] The promise of the revolution to create a wholly new society based on equality and social justice resonated far and wide. Nothing seemed out of reach. To quite a few people, however, the process looked more like pushing Russia through a meat-grinder. This ran against their deeply held values, beliefs, and principles. These people, some of them early enthusiasts themselves, were equally sincere in their rejection of Communist practices. Many decades later, descendants of the two groups continue this argument with the same sincerity and moral conviction.

There was also a Russia away from Russia: 3 million or so émigrés who fled abroad as a result of the revolution and the Civil War. These people, many of them true giants of literature (Nobel laureates Ivan Bunin and Vladimir Nabokov), philosophy (Nikolai Berdyaev), economics (Vasily Leontief), painting (Marc Chagall, Wassily Kandinsky), music (Feodor Chaliapin, Sergei Rakhmaninov, Igor Stravinsky), science, and technology (Ilya Prigozhin, Igor Sikorsky, Vladimir Zvorykin), sought to preserve the spirit of eternal Russia and the ideal of holiness that they associated with their motherland. It would only be in the late twentieth century that the incredibly rich legacy of Russian emigration would be made freely available to the people in Russia.

Meanwhile, Stalin, who emerged as a dictator, constructed a political system centered on the Communist Party apparatus that served as a pedestal and a tool for the leader; he radically transformed the country's economy by prioritizing heavy industry and turning peasants into agricultural laborers for the state; he replaced much of the old intelligentsia with a cadre schooled in the new Communist ideology; he turned the ideology itself into an equivalent of a religion, complete with dogmas, cults, rituals, and icons; and he maneuvered on the international scene in preparation for a war that was coming ever closer. In sum, while Lenin led the effort to do away with old Russia, Stalin built the Soviet state. That state would go through the hardest possible test of all, a war with Nazi Germany. And it would withstand that test.

3

World War II and Its Aftermath (1939–52)

Stalin's assessment that the 1938 Munich agreement was motivated by the desire of the Anglo-French "appeasers" to push Hitler's Germany eastward, ultimately to attack the Soviet Union, closed the book on the policy of collective security in Europe, which had been pursued by Moscow since 1933. In its place, Stalin decided on a two-track approach, which combined an outreach to Paris and London for a possible coalition against Germany, with a clear signal to Berlin of Moscow's desire to improve relations. In essence, Stalin was seeking to play one group of "capitalists," the democracies, against the other, the Nazis, while staying out of the fight himself. He may have also hoped that a new war among capitalist powers would create openings for the Comintern and the Soviet Union. War as a midwife to revolution was a set formula of Bolshevik thinking.

The Soviet–German Non-Aggression Pact and the Beginning of World War II

By the spring of 1939, Stalin came to the conclusion that it would make more sense for the Soviet Union to do a deal with Germany. He was under no illusion that the war with Hitler could be averted, but hoped to buy time to complete Soviet rearmament programs. Stalin accepted the German offer to negotiate a trade agreement between the two countries. At the same time, however, he proposed to Paris and London that the USSR, France, and Britain give joint military guarantees to Eastern European countries – Poland, Romania, and the Baltic States – against Germany. In case of a crisis, the Red Army would march through those countries' territories to Germany's borders to uphold or restore the status quo.

Warsaw and Bucharest, fearful of a de facto Soviet occupation, rejected this plan out of hand. Britain and France, who were mostly concerned with making sure that Germany didn't attack in the west, ostensibly wanted to find some compromise. Yet the military delegations they sent to Moscow in August dragged their feet and lacked the proper authority to conclude a military pact. It was at that moment that Stalin, who was in parallel negotiating with the Germans, finally decided in favor of an agreement with Hitler, whom he considered more interested in making the deal. Stalin pronounced the stalled talks with the Western powers terminated, and notified Berlin that he would welcome Hitler's envoy to the Kremlin.

On August 23, 1939, Molotov and Nazi foreign minister Joachim von Ribbentrop, in Stalin's presence, signed a Soviet–German non-aggression pact. Stalin believed he was buying time before the start of an inevitable war with Germany. He was also seeking to improve the Soviet Union's strategic position. Attached to the treaty was a secret protocol that delineated the respective spheres of influence of the two countries in Eastern Europe. The Soviet sphere extended to Estonia, Latvia, Finland, Bessarabia, and eastern Poland, mostly populated by ethnic Ukrainians and Belarusians. A month later, Lithuania was also added to this list. To Stalin, recovering the territory of the former Russian Empire meant advancing the Red Army positions by a few hundred kilometers westward, toward Germany.

On September 1, 1939, the German Wehrmacht invaded Poland, thus starting World War II. On September 17, the Red Army entered Poland from the east to take control of the territories assigned to the USSR under the secret protocol. The Poles offered the Soviets little resistance. Poland's eastern lands were promptly added to Soviet Ukraine and Belarus. During Ribbentrop's follow-up visit to Moscow in late September, the USSR and Germany finally agreed on their new border, which cut through what only recently used to be Poland. It now ran roughly along the ethnically based Curzon line proposed in 1919 by the then British foreign secretary as a Russo-Polish border. Eastern Europe was thus divided between Germany and the Soviet Union.

During the fall of 1939, the USSR proceeded with implementing the rest of the secret protocol. The Baltic States were made to sign treaties of mutual assistance with Moscow, which provided for the stationing of Soviet troops in their territory. Stalin,

however, needed full control of the region. By next
August, the three small countries had experienced
Soviet-engineered *coups d'état*, proclaimed themselves
Soviet republics, and were "admitted" to the USSR.
To eliminate a possible "fifth column" within the
expanded Soviet Union, tens of thousands of "bour-
geois elements" from Estonia, Latvia, and Lithuania
were deported to Siberia.

Soon thereafter, Moscow offered Helsinki a territorial swap. The Finnish border ran only 25 kilometers
north of Leningrad, which made the Soviet city vulnerable to long-range artillery fire. Stalin wanted to
push the border farther north, and offered the Finns
more territory elsewhere; he also demanded the right
to establish Soviet military bases in Finland. When in
late November 1939 the Finns rejected the offer, the
Red Army attacked Finland. The Finns fought bravely,
and the Soviet forces suffered heavy losses. Finally,
however, the latter managed, at a high cost, to break
through the Finnish defenses. The "Winter War," as
it is called in Finland, ended in March 1940. Finland
had to cede eastern Karelia, including the Karelian
Isthmus. Leningrad could feel safe. In July 1940,
the Soviet Union issued an ultimatum to Romania,
demanding that it cede Bessarabia, which it occupied
in 1918, and northern Bukovina. Duly abandoned by
its ally Berlin, Bucharest agreed. Thus, with the excep-
tion of Finland and Poland, the Soviet Union recovered all the territories of the Russian Empire that were
lost as a result of the revolution.

Stalin hoped that the "imperialist war" war between Germany and the Anglo-French coalition would last long enough for both sides to exhaust themselves. That would allow the USSR to complete its war preparations and step in at the last moment as an arbiter and a true winner. Meanwhile, Stalin was resolved not to give Hitler the slightest pretext for turning against the Soviet Union. He was also careful not to be provoked by British warnings of a coming German attack against the USSR. Soviet propaganda duly presented Germany as a "peace-loving nation" and the Western allies as "aggressors"; the fate of Poland was hardly mourned. The Soviet Union supplied Germany with agricultural produce and various raw materials. A number of German Communists who had sought refuge in the Soviet Union were even handed over to the Gestapo. However, the Soviet military continued to prepare for war with Germany, although it envisaged a different conflict to the one that actually took place. Stalin expected the Red Army's campaign to be offensive, swift, and victorious.

The calculation was wrong, but for reasons largely outside of Stalin's control. Stalin was surprised first by the phoney war in the west that saw virtually no military action, then by France's quick and catastrophic collapse, Britain's inability to help its continental allies, and Germany's almost effortless occupation of many European countries. By May 1940, after the fall of Paris and the débâcle at Dunkirk, he certainly understood that the Soviet Union would be next on Hitler's hit list. Moreover, now Germany's power had grown tremendously: it could rely on the support of virtually the entire industrial and manpower resources of the European continent. Trying to buy more time became a more desperate exercise for the Kremlin.

For his part, Hitler, who had always wanted Germany to expand all the way to the east and crush and destroy Russia, tried to engage Stalin in a deceptive game of his own. In the fall of 1940, he offered the Soviet Union to join the Axis powers and take part in the dismemberment of British India. Stalin responded by dispatching Molotov to Berlin.[1] While carefully avoiding the India issue, Stalin demanded a sphere of influence for the Soviet Union all the way from Finland to Bulgaria and from the Caucasus to the Persian Gulf, including a military base in the Turkish Straits, as well as southern Sakhalin. The Soviet leader still hoped to win time by bargaining with his main adversary. He placed his bet on the notion that before taking on the USSR, Germany would still need to defeat Britain. He was wrong.

Germany Attacks the Soviet Union

Hitler did not care to respond: in December 1940, a month after Molotov's visit, he approved a plan of a *Blitzkrieg* against the Soviet Union. The plan, code-named *Barbarossa*, foresaw a defeat of the Soviet Union within 100 days and occupation of the entire European territory of Russia all the way to the line from Archangel on the White Sea to Astrakhan on the Caspian. On June 22, 1941, the German Wehrmacht invaded the Soviet Union along the front stretching from the Baltic to the Black Sea. Stalin, who, despite the intelligence he was getting, had firmly believed Hitler would not attack in 1941, was completely taken by surprise. The Soviet forces, which had trained to attack Germany at the right moment, rather than to defend their own territory, suffered enormous losses.

Yet, even in retreat, and despite the expectations of many in the West, Soviet troops offered surprisingly strong resistance, which critically slowed the Wehrmacht's advance. The border fortress in Brest held out for longer than a month; Soviet warplanes bombed Berlin already in July 1941; and Soviet troops even counter-attacked on the road to Moscow. Heroism became a mass phenomenon. All this was in stark contrast to what the Germans had encountered on the western front. Contrary to many expert predictions, Soviet forces were not collapsing. The patriotic effort on the front line was supported by the entire country.

In a unique and virtually miraculous exercise of Soviet economic war management, the bulk of the country's heavy industry, located in the country's western regions, was evacuated, lock, stock, and barrel, a thousand or more kilometers eastward, to Siberia and the Urals. Within a few weeks, these plants and factories were operating again. The Soviet government did not crack; there was no palace coup in the Kremlin.

Stalin did not leave Moscow even as the front line was fast approaching the Kremlin, and did not sue for peace. The Russian people did not rise against the Soviet regime, brutal as it was. Instead, the German attack reignited Russian patriotism, which immediately turned the war into a fight for the motherland, with Stalin as its prime defender. Communist dogma had to take the back seat for the duration of the war.

The Wehrmacht managed to seize the Baltics, Belarus, Ukraine, and Moldova, and by the fall and early winter of 1941 it reached the gates of Leningrad, Moscow, and Rostov. Yet by that time its drive had run out of steam. Russia's enormous strategic depth played its role again. The Red Army got a second wind when it was able to deploy fresh divisions from Siberia – when it became clear that Japan was not going to attack the USSR in the Far East. Cold weather was also punishing the attackers, who had not calculated that the war would last into the winter months. In early December 1941, the German forces, which had come within 28 kilometers of the Kremlin, were pushed back by 150 to 200 kilometers. That was the first strategic success for the Soviet Union. *Barbarossa* and the *Blitzkrieg* had failed.

The Great Patriotic War

Stalin, reflecting the spirit of the people, proclaimed a Great Patriotic War, on the model of the 1812 defense against Napoleon. He also put it in the historical context of Russian struggle for independence from many foreign aggressors, from the Teutonic knights and the Mongol hordes to the Polish, Swedish, and French armies. In his speeches, Stalin evoked the memories of Russian war leaders from previous centuries, and instituted military decorations named after them. For him, as for his successors, Russian history would be a resource of moral strength, particularly *in extremis*. Driven by necessity, Stalin also reversed his stance on the Russian Orthodox Church. In 1943, he invited its surviving leaders to the Kremlin and permitted the church to operate again, within the limits he set himself. In the same year, he closed down the Comintern and replaced the *Internationale* with a new national anthem praising Russia as the core of the Soviet Union. Faced with the existential threat, the Soviet state was becoming more cohesive.

The Soviet–German war from beginning to end was part of World War II. Right after the German attack on the Soviet Union, Winston Churchill and Franklin D. Roosevelt announced their countries' support for the USSR. In doing this, they immediately put aside their vehement rejection of Communist theory and practice. An anti-Hitler coalition began to emerge, singularly focused on defeating the common enemy of Great Britain, the Soviet Union, and the United States. America, not yet formally at war with the Axis powers, offered the Soviet Union military and other aid under the Lend-Lease Act. The USSR acceded to the Atlantic Charter.

The Soviet–German front became the principal battle line of World War II. It saw the greatest concentration of land forces during the war (two-thirds of the Wehrmacht were deployed there), the highest loss of life, and probably the biggest human suffering. The toll from the 900-day-long siege of Leningrad (1941–4) alone amounted to nearly 1 million dead. In late 1942, the Soviet forces stopped the Wehrmacht's offensive at Stalingrad on the Volga, and by early 1943 they crushed the German forces there. The epic battle for Stalingrad marked the turning point in the war. The frontline started moving westward.

On the Road to Victory

In July 1943, Germany undertook its last major offensive on the eastern front, near Kursk, which was again crushed by the Soviet counter-offensive. The Battle of the Kursk Bulge saw the biggest tank battle in history (over 1,200 vehicles), at Prokhorovka. From then on, the Red Army was only advancing. In November 1943, it crossed the Dnieper River and entered Kiev. In January 1944, the siege of Leningrad was broken. In July 1944, as the allies landed on the Normandy beaches, Soviet forces liberated Minsk. By the end of that year, German forces had been driven from the Soviet territory they occupied in 1941: Ukraine, Belarus, the Baltics, and Moldova.

The Red Army now crossed into Poland, Slovakia, Romania, and Bulgaria. Finland, which, as a German ally, fought its own "continuation war" against the USSR from 1941 to 1944, sued for peace. So did Romania, which had sent forces to fight against the Soviets, like Hungary, Italy, and Spain. While the war still raged, the next big issue was the post-war organization of Europe, and the world. The Soviet Union was getting ready to capitalize diplomatically on the successes of its military forces. After the experience of 1813–15, this would be the second time when Russia's successful defense of the motherland would lead it all the way to the aggressor's capital and allow it to jointly decide the post-war order in Europe.

The Big Three (Churchill, Roosevelt, and Stalin) held summit conferences in Tehran in November 1943 and in Yalta in February 1945. The conferences, lasting three and seven days, respectively, allowed for detailed discussions. Stalin proved himself a skillful diplomat. Relying on the critical importance of the Soviet war effort for future allied victory, he managed to protect Soviet geopolitical interests and won a number of concessions from his counterparts. At Yalta in particular, the Soviet leader essentially won an understanding by America and Britain for the Soviet Union's need for a measure of influence in Eastern Europe.

The future political orientation of Poland was a particularly thorny issue. Stalin insisted on a "friendly" – i.e., pro-Soviet – Poland that would be a strong buffer state between the Soviet Union and post-war Germany. Britain and the United States, for their part, wanted to keep Poland as a democratic Western-leaning country on the Soviet border. Each party was backing its own group of Polish politicians and armed groups vying for power. To a lesser degree, similar conflicts emerged in other newly liberated countries, including Czechoslovakia, Hungary, Romania, Bulgaria, and Greece.

On May 2, 1945, after heavy fighting that cost 100,000 Soviet soldiers' lives, the Red Army took Berlin. Hitler had committed suicide two days before. The Soviet red flag over the Reichstag building symbolized the triumph. On May 8, the German forces surrendered unconditionally. In the Soviet Union, May 9 was declared the Day of Victory. At the two-week conference in Potsdam in July–August 1945, with Harry S. Truman replacing the deceased Roosevelt, and Clement Attlee taking over from Churchill midway after a UK general election, the three powers decided how to jointly run Germany, and manage post-war Europe. Managing the new world order fell to the United Nations, which was founded at the same time. The USSR became a permanent veto-wielding member of the UN Security Council, one of the five "global policemen," in Roosevelt's words.

1945 in Russian Memory

To this day, victory in the Great Patriotic War that culminated in the defeat of Nazism is regarded in Russia as its biggest contribution to humanity. This is part of Russia's current identity and is unlikely to change.

Despite the enormous losses and damage caused by the war, Russians do not see Germans as hereditary enemies. They managed to separate in their minds Germans and Nazism. Victory in 1945 has allowed Russians to see Germans as co-equals, so that they, unlike many Europeans, do not fear a resurgent Germany.

However, any attempt to question the role that the USSR played in World War II is widely seen as a vicious anti-Russian attack. The memory of the war dead is sacred. It is still not known exactly how many people perished. The official count now stands at 26.6 million, of whom about 8.7 million were servicemen,[2] and the rest, civilians. May 9 is thus a day of both celebration and remembrance. This is not fading away with time. The "immortal regiment" parade of ordinary people marching in the streets on that day carrying portraits of their relatives who fought in the war has recently become a feature across the country.

The victory had many sources. Certainly, Russian patriotism and a capacity for perseverance played a major role. The military, decimated during the pre-war purges and having absorbed a seemingly crushing blow in the first six months of the war, managed to transform itself into a formidable force. Economic mobilization was a great feat: essentially, the Soviet Union managed to out-produce Germany in terms of weaponry and war materiel. Assistance under the Lend-Lease program was important, particularly when it came to trucks and other land vehicles and aircraft. Strong leadership and discipline kept the country together in the bleakest moments, but essentially the war was won by the people as a whole, not just by Stalin and his marshals.

Post-war Reconstruction and Recentralization

With the war over, Soviet people began rebuilding their devastated country. Many cities – Stalingrad, Voronezh, Sevastopol – were completely destroyed, and hundreds of others lay in ruins. Industrial and transport infrastructure were badly damaged. The main task was to restore and reconstruct what was lost in the war. Within five years, as a result of a major effort, this task was largely completed. Particularly difficult was rebuilding agriculture: the country's main agricultural areas happened to be in the war zone. In 1947, drought, lack of labor and equipment, and administrative mismanagement led to a famine – the last in Russia's history.

Stalin, for his part, was busy restoring the symbols of the Russian Empire. By 1945, Soviet borders embraced virtually all of the tsarist realm, except for Finland and Poland. People's commissars were again called ministers; military officers were issued shoulder boards with traditional insignia and the Red Army was renamed the Soviet Army; and the rehabilitated Orthodox Church was once more allowed to elect a patriarch of Moscow and all Russia. Post-revolutionary émigrés were invited to return to the Soviet Union. Capitalist America and Britain were official allies. Stalin supported the creation of the State of Israel and considered establishing a Jewish homeland in Crimea. The emerging post-war "relaxation," however, was very superficial and short-lived.

Sowing the Seeds of the Cold War

World War II turned the Soviet Union into a world power. Germany was divided into four zones, with the USSR occupying its eastern part, including East Berlin. Soviet forces also occupied eastern Austria, including Vienna, while part of East Prussia with Koenigsberg, renamed Kaliningrad, became a Soviet province. The Soviet territorial acquisitions of 1939–40 were internationally recognized.[3] By 1948, Eastern European countries – Poland, Czechoslovakia, Hungary, Romania, Bulgaria, and Albania – were turned into Soviet satellites. In Asia, a Communist victory in the civil war turned China in 1949 into a Soviet ally. North Korea and North Vietnam were also controlled by the local Communist parties, and Port Arthur, lost to Japan in 1905, was again a Russian naval base. Stalin's writ extended from Potsdam to Pyongyang. Never since Genghis Khan has any ruler controlled so much of the mega-continent of Eurasia.

This expansion of the Kremlin's power was not unopposed. The Soviet Union's relations with the

Western allies became progressively tense. Already from 1945, each saw the other as a geopolitical rival and an ideological adversary. The use of US nuclear weapons against Japan was interpreted in Moscow as a warning to the Soviet Union. Stalin's and Churchill's 1946 speeches[4] signaled the start of what was soon called the Cold War.[5] By 1948, confrontation was official. A crisis over Western access to Berlin, deep inside the Soviet occupation zone, for the first time pitted the wartime allies against each other. NATO was formed in the same year, with the United States formally guaranteeing for the first time the security of Western European countries. In East Asia, Chinese Communists, with Soviet support, established their rule in mainland China, while in 1950, Stalin allowed Kim Il Sung to start a war to bring South Korea under Communist control.[6]

To end the US atomic monopoly, Stalin ordered a major effort to build Soviet nuclear weapons. The physicist Igor Kurchatov was appointed the scientific director of the project, and the security chief Lavrentiy Beria was put in overall charge. Soviet spies active in the United States provided priceless intelligence on the US program. In 1949, the first Soviet A-bomb was successfully tested in Kazakhstan. About three years later, the USSR tested its first hydrogen bomb, roughly at the same time as the United States. One of its creators was Andrei Sakharov, the future leading Soviet dissident and democratic politician. Missiles and aircraft were produced on a large scale – in anticipation of a new war with the US-led capitalist West which Stalin considered inevitable.

Domestic Repression

Stalin also faced domestic challenges. The war-ravaged country had to be rebuilt. This required another major effort and serious sacrifice. The Cold War, while giving Moscow access to the resources of East Germany and Czechoslovakia, severed the Soviet Union's economic ties with advanced Western countries. The Lend-Lease program was discontinued immediately after the end of the war. The Marshall Plan was designed in such a way as to preclude Soviet membership – although Stalin was suspicious of its objectives from the start. Yet within five years basic reconstruction of the country was accomplished. At the same time, the Soviet Union had to bear the burden of supporting a number of new allies. The greatest amount of assistance was given between 1949 and 1959 to the People's Republic of China. The foundation of China's heavy industry, including its defense sector, was laid then.

There were other challenges. During the war, Russian people gained new experience. On the battlefield, they were often left one on one with the enemy and had to make decisions on their own; qualities such as fortitude, personal valor, and loyalty to friends and family overshadowed ideology and sycophancy so widespread in peacetime; and while

Communist ideology had to take a back seat, religious faith made a stunning resurgence. In their pursuit of the Wehrmacht, Soviet citizens in uniform also saw a number of foreign countries, and were impressed by the living standards and the way of life that they found in Central and Eastern Europe, which contrasted starkly with the squalid conditions to which they had been accustomed at home.

Stalin saw this and made his own conclusions. He moved against the top military chiefs, including the famous Marshal Zhukov, whom he considered potential rivals as principal makers of victory. They were sent to command distant military districts. Decades later, in his epitaph on Zhukov's death, the poet Joseph Brodsky wrote about Soviet generals who "bravely entered alien capitals, but feared to return to their own." Already in 1946, Stalin ordered that the Day of Victory in the Great Patriotic War would no longer be a public holiday. A number of military officers and civilians who privately expressed criticism of Stalin's leadership were jailed, like Captain Alexander Solzhenitsyn, or shot. The post-war wave of repression affected cultural figures such as the poet Anna Akhmatova and the composer Dmitri Shostakovich, who were publicly censured. Marriages between Soviet citizens and foreigners were banned.

In 1949, Stalin turned 70. The celebration marked the culmination of his cult. In the remaining years of his life, even as his physical and mental health degraded, there was a paroxysm of repression. During that period, the dictator directed his most cruel blows against the groups whom he considered particularly dangerous to his rule: the ethnic Russian Soviet bureaucracy, whom he, as a non-Russian, suspected of nationalism; and the Jewish intelligentsia, who held key positions in science, technology, medicine, and the arts. Stalin probably feared nothing more than an alliance between those two groups. And he resolved to suppress them.

The so-called "Leningrad case" resulted in the execution in 1950 of the chief Soviet economic planner, Nikolai Voznesensky, Central Committee secretary Alexei Kuznetsov, and the Leningrad party chief, Pyotr Popkov, as well as dozens of other senior party and government officials, almost exclusively ethnic Russians. Tens of thousands of others were jailed, banished, or demoted. Stalin feared that these people, who after the war considered improving the livelihoods of ordinary people their top priority, might steer the country away from his policies that prioritized the state and the empire. A mere suspicion that the "plotters" considered establishing Leningrad as the capital of the Russian republic (in the USSR, Moscow doubled as both the Soviet and Russian capital) carried the threat of duality of power, which would tear the Soviet Union apart.[7] Actually, this is precisely what happened four decades later, as the Russian republic President Boris Yeltsin entered into a stand-off with Soviet President Mikhail Gorbachev, which resulted in the break-up of the USSR.

In 1952, Stalin began implementing a succession plan when he expanded the party leadership by including within it a number of younger people, such as Leonid Brezhnev and Alexei Kosygin. The idea was probably to get these protégés up to speed before physically eliminating the old guard: Georgi Malenkov, Molotov, Beria, and others. Molotov later confided that had Stalin lived a year or two longer, he, Molotov, would probably have been executed. Things turned out differently, however.

January 1953 saw Stalin's attack against the Jews reach its culmination in his campaign against the so-called "Doctors' Plot." Right after the war, the Jewish Anti-Fascist Committee had been disbanded, some of its members, like the actor Solomon Mikhoels, had been assassinated, and others, including Molotov's wife, had been banished. What started as a preventive strike against prominent Jews degenerated into full-blown paranoia. Two months before his death, Stalin unleashed a campaign against Kremlin doctors who were treating top party figures, including himself. When his health sharply deteriorated, his bodyguards were too terrified to call the doctors. Beria reportedly admitted responsibility for denying Stalin medical assistance, but the true circumstances of the dictator's death will probably never be known. Whatever the truth, Stalin died on March 5, 1953.

The human toll of the repressions he had launched was horrendous. Exact numbers are disputed, but whatever numbers one uses, the scale of suffering was enormous. The first official count prepared for Nikita Khrushchev less than a year after Stalin's death put the number of those convicted of counter-revolutionary crimes between 1921 and 1953 at 3,777,380, of whom 642,980 were sentenced to death.[8] Other figures used by various historians were much higher. According to some, between 1929 and 1953, 883,000 people were executed as "counter-revolutionaries." Estimates say that roughly every sixth adult Soviet citizen was directly affected by the machine of terror operated by the secret police. About 18–20 million are believed to have gone through the GULAG system, and 7 million were banished or exiled. Repression did not pause even during the war. Soviet POWs, once liberated, were often transferred to the GULAG: their crime was having allowed themselves to become POWs in the first place. Whole ethnic groups – Chechens, Ingush, Crimean Tartars, Karachai, Kalmyks, Meskhetian Turks, and others – were made collectively responsible for their co-ethnics who sided with the Nazis and were banished, mostly to Central Asia. A large portion of the victims never survived the deportation. In 1940, over 10,000 Polish officers and civilians were executed at Katyn and other camps in central Russia.

Stalin's legacy

To this day, Stalin remains a most controversial figure in Russia. As long as he ruled, he was adulated as a *vozhd*, a great leader and even a "father of nations." Soon after he died, he was officially condemned for his crimes and his cult of personality, and remained a virtual non-person for a decade. Later, his name was allowed to be occasionally mentioned in public, and curiously became a symbol of quiet grass-roots protest against elite corruption. In the late 1980s, glasnost appeared to have completely discredited Stalin, but from the 1990s his name became a symbol for all those who opposed liberal policies, from Communists to nationalists. As of this writing, Stalin is probably the most popular Russian leader of all time and his leadership in the Great Patriotic War is seen as his greatest achievement.

This is the core reason for Stalin's popularity among many Russians. He designed and built the Soviet state; he led its defense in the most excruciating experience of the Great Patriotic War, never leaving Moscow even when the frontline came within two dozen kilometers of the Kremlin; and he disciplined the elites, mostly by harsh measures, while providing a crude semblance of order within the country. Those Russians who value people's lives and people's rights above the power of the state, of course, vehemently disagree. They consider Stalin absolutely the worst person ever to rule Russia. As Stalin's period ceases to be part of living memory, the crimes committed by him and his henchmen are increasingly viewed as part of history, never to be repeated but reflecting not so much the evil intentions of Stalin and other individuals as the tragedy of Russian society in the era of wars and revolutions which destroyed the sanctity of life and debased its value.

4

Mature Socialism and Its Stagnation (1953–84)

The death of the dictator led to a power struggle between his would-be successors, just as it had
thirty years before. Indeed this remained a feature
of the Soviet political system till its very end. Nikita
Khrushchev, far from the obvious heir to Stalin – like
Stalin himself after Lenin – managed to defeat his
rivals. He did this in three stages. In the summer of
1953, Khrushchev and all his colleagues in the party
leadership came together against Beria, the ambitious
former state security chief, whom they saw as a mortal
danger to all. As a result, Beria was arrested in the
Kremlin and soon executed. This was the last execution of a major political figure in Russia. In 1955,
Khrushchev, by that time the party's first secretary, outmaneuvered Malenkov, and replaced him as premier,
considered the top job. In the final move, in 1957,
Khrushchev sacked still influential Molotov and the
war hero and powerful defense minister Zhukov to
establish complete control over the party and government. As in the 1920s, so it was again in the 1960s;
collective leadership did not last long.

Stalin's Cult Destroyed

Khrushchev was directly implicated in Stalin's crimes and bore responsibility for mass repression. Yet he was a very different personality from Stalin. He sincerely believed in Communist ideals and sought to turn them into Soviet reality. However, he realized that the mass killings, the GULAG legacy, and deportations carried out during Stalin's long reign were too heavy a burden to carry forward. He therefore made a bold decision to condemn these crimes. In 1956, to the consternation of the delegates to the 20th Congress of the Communist Party of the Soviet Union (CPSU) assembled in the Kremlin, he presented a report on "Stalin's cult of personality and its consequences." The report produced an emotional earthquake in the Soviet Union and sent shock waves across the Communist world.

At the same time, Khrushchev made an effort to ascribe these "distortions of socialism" to Stalin personally, and to the security organs, while exonerating the party as a victim. He limited the revelations to the period between Kirov's murder in 1934 and Stalin's death in 1953, and focused in particular on two years of Great Terror, 1937 and 1938, when Stalin was physically eliminating the Bolshevik old guard and the senior leadership of the Armed Forces. The millions of victims of collectivization, the famine, the war on religion, not to speak of the Red Terror during the Civil War, were not included in Khrushchev's indictment. For him, what was done before 1934 was basically justified; and Lenin, who now remained the single personal symbol of the Soviet Communist system, had to remain absolutely sacred. Even this partial cleansing, however, was enormously positive. To this day, it stands as Khrushchev's most important achievement, and a mark of his personal courage: many of his colleagues in the leadership resisted the destruction of "the cult."

Khrushchev's words were followed by actions. Stalin was almost physically dethroned, his body taken out of the mausoleum in Red Square and buried near the Kremlin wall. His countless monuments were removed, except for one, in his native town of Gori, in Georgia. Stalingrad became Volgograd; Stalino, Donetsk; Stalin (in Bulgaria), Varna. In 1956, the remaining 800,000 GULAG prisoners were released. State security organs were reformed, with many of the cadres replaced by younger and better-educated men. The KGB, as the new security agency was called, was placed under the control of the Communist Party apparatus, and no longer closely monitored the senior members of the party *nomenklatura*. This allowed party functionaries to breathe a sigh of relief for the first time since the 1917 revolution. At last, they were able to feel safe within the system that they themselves had created.

Economic and Social Revival

Khrushchev was both ambitious and energetic. Convinced of the great potential of socialism, he set the goal of "overtaking and surpassing the United States" in key economic areas. In 1961, he proclaimed the coming age of abundance – he called it "Communism" – which he promised would become a reality in the USSR by 1980. Indeed, since the mid-1950s, the Soviet economy had experienced a surge. Volga sedans and TU-104 turbojet passenger planes became symbols of technological progress. For the first time since the NEP, Soviet industry expanded the production of consumer goods: TV sets, refrigerators, and washing machines. The world was also stunned when in 1957 the first orbital satellite, Sputnik, was launched, followed in 1961 by the first man in space, Yuri Gagarin, and in 1963 by the first woman in space, Valentina Tereshkova. At universities, natural sciences and mathematics were prioritized. New centers of science were built from scratch, like Dubna near Moscow and Akademgorodok in Novosibirsk.

Khrushchev dreamt of modern large-scale mechanized agriculture. He ordered the development of vast virgin lands in Kazakhstan, insisted on the mass planting of corn, and on using chemical fertilizers. He promoted the elimination of small villages in favor of big ones, and severely restricted what collective farmers were allowed to keep or cultivate individually. Some of these measures resulted in short-term gains, while others, often thoughtlessly implemented, like growing corn north of the Arctic Circle, were disastrous. These were compounded by a bad harvest. In 1963, the Soviet Union, for the first time in history, started the practice of importing grain from abroad. Ultimately, the inability of the Soviet system to provide a reliable supply of staple food across the country became one of the main reasons for the popular discontent that undermined Communist rule.

Khrushchev believed that the rising incomes of ordinary people would be the best argument for Communism. Probably his biggest social policy initiative was the building of new houses for urban dwellers, many of whom had had to live for decades in basements or communal apartments where 10 to 20 tenants would share a single bathroom. For the first time since the revolution, new apartment blocks were built for average Soviet people, not the *nomenklatura* or the elites. Labor conditions improved: the working day was limited to seven hours, and the working week to six days, pensions were increased, and taxes were lowered. Control of peasants' movements was relaxed. Kindergartens were built, abortions were legalized, and mass sports and internal tourism were promoted. Seaside vacations in Crimea and the Caucasus became widely available. The number of students and young professionals grew. Deported ethnic groups, such as the Chechens and Kalmyks, were allowed to return from internal exile. However, these positive developments were marred in 1962 by the army's bloody suppression of food protests in the southern Russian city of Novocherkassk, resulting in at least 25 deaths.

The "Thaw"

The first post-Stalin decade is known as the "thaw," owing to the cultural and intellectual liberalization that took place. *Novy Mir* (New World), a literary journal edited by the writer Alexander Tvardovsky, began to publish works that offered an unvarnished view of Soviet realities. In 1962, it printed Alexander Solzhenitsyn's *One Day in the Life of Ivan Denisovich*, a vivid account of GULAG realities. Works by Russian authors, such as Fyodor Dostoevsky or Sergei Yesenin, effectively banned under Stalin, were again made available. A whole generation of free-thinking writers, film directors, intellectuals, and the like, emerged. The poets Yevgeny Yevtushenko, Andrei Voznesensky, Bella Akhmadulina, Joseph Brodsky, and Robert Rozhdestvensky; the writer Vasily Aksyonov; and the filmmaker Marlen Khutsiev, among others, were collectively called "the people of the '60s." This was also the time of the rise of Soviet scientific fantasy novels, as represented by the Strugatsky brothers, Arkady and Boris, best known for their *Roadside Picnic* (1972), which was later filmed as *Stalker* (1979) by Andrei Tarkovsky. This breath of fresh air would not be extinguished till the end of Communist rule.

In 1955, the Kremlin was opened for visitors for

the first time since the Soviet leadership moved to live there in 1918. (The leadership had moved out since.) In 1957, Moscow hosted a world youth festival, which brought 30,000 young foreigners to the Soviet Union. In 1964, the still largely closed country welcomed 1 million tourists, while thousands of Soviet specialists were sent to work abroad, mostly to Asian and African countries, where the Soviet Union was building plants, dams, and roads. Cultural and scientific exchanges with the West became frequent, as the Bolshoi and Kirov ballet companies toured the world, and Soviet scientists began to attend international conferences. After the Soviet Union's debut in the 1952 Olympics, sports links expanded greatly. In 1956, the Soviet football team won an Olympic gold; in 1960, Soviet soccer players became champions of Europe.

The thaw, however, had its limits. Boris Pasternak's novel *Doctor Zhivago*, which was published abroad in 1957 and won the Nobel Literature Prize the following year, was condemned as anti-Soviet; Pasternak was subjected to a vicious defamation campaign, which hastened his demise (he died in 1960). In 1962, Khrushchev raged against avant-garde art at an exhibition in the Manezh Hall. He publicly yelled at the poet Andrei Voznesensky and the sculptor Ernst Neizvestny, accusing them of being anti-Soviet. From 1958, Khrushchev had launched a full-scale attack on religion, which he thought had no place in the Communist society he was building. After *One*

Day in the Life of Ivan Denisovich, further works by Solzhenitsyn were banned. Russian readers could still read them in *samizdat* (self-published) and *tamizdat* (foreign published) copies, however, and unlike in Stalin's time, this no longer carried the risk of execution or incarceration. Large-scale repression was not revived. Khrushchev was often despised, but never feared. His sycophants' attempts to create a cult of sorts around the figure of the new top leader were met with cynicism. *Anekdoty* – fictitious funny stories – about Khrushchev became ubiquitous, which would have been unthinkable in the days of Stalin.

Khrushchev's Defense and Foreign Policy

In the field of defense, Khrushchev banked on new technology, first of all ballistic missiles, which could carry a nuclear warhead and from 1957 were capable of reaching US territory. The missile program and its space offspring were led by Sergei Korolev. In 1961, the Soviet Union exploded the world's most powerful nuclear device. These advances in technology, which led to the creation in 1959 of the Strategic Rocket Force as a separate military service in the Soviet armed forces, allowed Krushchev to carry out a massive reduction in the army and navy. The numbers of soldiers, airmen, and sailors went down from 5 million in 1955 to 3 million in 1958. In 1960, another reduction by 1 million men was announced. These massive reductions, not accompanied by retraining or rehabilitation programs for the prematurely retired officers, bred resentment, which would help anti-Khrushchev plotters a few years later.

Soviet foreign policy of the period was still built on the notion of class struggle against "world imperialism led by the United States," but it also professed a desire for peaceful coexistence with the West. Immediately after Stalin's death, the new leadership embraced a policy of détente – the first one in the Cold War. In July 1953, an armistice stopped the Korean War. In 1954, the leaders of the Soviet Union, the United States, Britain, and France met in Geneva for the first time since World War II to discuss the German Question. In 1955, Austria was restored as a neutral state, its occupation ended. Khrushchev quickly developed a taste for personal diplomacy. He became the first Soviet leader to travel widely – to Britain in 1956, the United States in 1959, France in 1960, but also to India, Indonesia, Egypt, Yugoslavia, and other non-aligned countries. In 1955, West German chancellor Konrad Adenauer came to Moscow, and in 1956, so did the Japanese prime minister. The state of war was ended with both Germany and Japan. Meanwhile, Molotov, who embodied Stalinist foreign policy, was sacked, and soon replaced by Andrei Gromyko, who stayed in the job till the days of Mikhail Gorbachev.

In relation to the countries of the "socialist camp," Moscow pursued a policy of consolidation and, when necessary, repression. In 1955, in response to West Germany's inclusion within NATO, the Soviet Union organized a military bloc of its own, the Warsaw Pact, to which Poland, the GDR, Hungary, Czechoslovakia, Romania, Bulgaria, and Albania belonged. Increasingly, the USSR had to subsidize its Eastern European satellites. This tutelage began to encounter resistance. In 1953, the Soviet garrison brutally crushed an uprising of East Berlin workers who protested against a reduction of wages accompanied by a hike in production norms. In 1956, Khrushchev had to deal with popular uprisings in the satellite countries as a consequence of his de-Stalinization campaign. He ordered a massive use of force to put down Hungary's attempt to break away from the Warsaw Pact. He also threatened Poland, which was experiencing popular disturbances of its own, with a Soviet intervention. The threat worked. Finally, in 1961, to stop the dangerous outflow of East Germans to the West via the open border in Berlin, Khrushchev sanctioned the building of a wall in the divided city. In all instances, the West stayed put, grudgingly respecting the Cold War divide.

A breakthrough occurred in the Soviet Union's relations with the countries of Asia, Africa, and Latin America amid the process of de-colonization there. From the mid-1950s, Moscow became increasingly involved in the Middle East. In the 1956 Suez crisis, it issued an ultimatum to Britain, France, and Israel. The Soviet nuclear threat halted the three powers' intervention. Within a few years, Egypt and Algeria, India and Indonesia, Mali and Guinea became outposts of Soviet influence in what was termed the "Third World." Foreign economic assistance to "countries seeking a non-capitalist path of development" became an item in the Soviet budget. In 1960, moreover, the Soviet Union befriended revolutionary Cuba, which soon became the focal point of the most dangerous nuclear confrontation in the history of the Cold War.

To protect Cuba from a US military intervention, and to balance the deployment of US nuclear missiles in Turkey and Italy, Khrushchev decided in 1962 to install Soviet missiles in Cuba. The operation which he launched was undertaken in utter secrecy. When the Americans discovered what was going on, Gromyko was told to lie in President John F. Kennedy's face. The United States, fearing an imminent attack, was preparing to wipe out the Soviet systems in Cuba, some of which were already operational (although the Americans were unaware of this). An all-out nuclear war was a distinct possibility. Fortunately, both Kennedy and Khrushchev found a way to de-escalate. The Soviet missiles were withdrawn from Cuba, followed by the US ones from Europe, and Cuba was allowed to experiment with its own version of socialism. In 1963, the United States, the Soviet Union, and Britain signed a treaty to ban all nuclear tests – except those underground: another détente amid the ongoing Cold War. Stepping away from the brink was fully supported by the Russian people. From the 1960s through to the 1980s, fear of a nuclear war was perhaps the biggest concern of ordinary Russians.

Yevgeny Yevtushenko expressed this very vividly in his 1961 poem "Do the Russians Want War?"

Khrushchev managed a partial reconciliation with Josip Broz Tito's Yugoslavia, which had strayed away from the Soviet bloc, but relations with China rapidly deteriorated – despite the huge economic assistance given by the USSR to the People's Republic in the 1950s. Mao Zedong, who both revered and feared Stalin, was angry with Khrushchev for his de-Stalinization. Moreover, Mao did not think much of the new Soviet leader and considered himself Stalin's true heir. Mao roundly rejected Khrushchev's attempt to treat China as a little Communist brother; he vehemently opposed the Soviet leader's outreach to the United States; and he saw Moscow's plan for creating a joint Soviet–Chinese submarine fleet as an inadmissible attack on China's sovereignty. In 1960, when Khrushchev had had enough, he recalled Soviet advisers and specialists from China, ushering in a three-decades-long period of cold war between the two Communist countries.

The Coup Against Khrushchev; the Collective Leadership Revisited

Foreign policy failures combined with rising domestic challenges, but above all it was Khrushchev's impatient, impetuous leadership style that led to a coup mounted against him by his own associates. Khrushchev's "voluntarism" – the official accusation against him – is still remembered to this day. His sudden transfer of Crimea from the Russian republic to Soviet Ukraine in 1954 was long held up as one of the prime examples of his misdeeds. In 1964, when Khrushchev was on vacation on the Black Sea, the party's senior figures, with broad support from the *nomenklatura* and with wide popular connivance or approval, ousted him. Khrushchev was retired to his dacha outside Moscow, where he died in 1971, age 77. With that, Soviet political culture made another step along the path of humanization. Stalin's rivals were murdered; Khrushchev's, demoted; Khrushchev himself was merely pensioned off, although officially he became a non-person.

As in the two previous successions – Lenin's in 1924 and Stalin's in 1953 – the disappearance of the top leader led to a collective leadership. Also as in these other two cases, it did not last long. By 1967, Leonid Brezhnev, the party general secretary, initially considered a transitional figure, emerged as the principal. Alexei Kosygin, the prime minister, acquiesced in his more junior position. The third member of the original troika, Nikolai Podgorny, the head of the Supreme Soviet, and thus the formal head of state, remained a nominal member of the leadership until his job was taken over by Brezhnev in 1977. More important, however, was the rise of the power of the Central Committee's 12- to 15-member Politburo. Brezhnev did not turn out to be a dictator like Stalin or a personalist leader like Khrushchev. While much, particularly in the later years, was done in his name, he was more of a *primus inter pares*. Momentous decisions such as the interventions in Czechoslovakia and Afghanistan, détente with the United States, or major weapons deployments were decided by the Politburo.

Brezhnev's Soviet Golden Age

Brezhnev was essentially a consensual person who frankly espoused a live-and-let-live philosophy. The issue, however, was not his personality. The Soviet system had outlived the Stalinist regime of a great leader reaching out to the common people and keeping the *nomenklatura* in constant fear of repression. Khrushchev's rule in this scheme of things was a temporary, and utterly unsuccessful, personalist regime. Brezhnev, by contrast, represented a new model that provided safety and security to the *nomenklatura*; a measure of affluence to the bulk of the population; a notional foundation for ideological rigor and unspoken freedom for "silent" dissent; and a foreign policy of "détente through military strength." In a phrase: guns and butter.

With consensus achieved at the top of the pyramid, dissent appeared where it never was able to publicly surface before: in the liberal intelligentsia quarters, among the so-called "dissidents." The removal of Khrushchev also marked the end of the "thaw." The new leadership did not restore Stalinism, but it stopped denunciation of Stalin and his regime: unlike

Khrushchev, they did not need it to legitimize their power; and they also considered rocking the boat any further dangerous for the Soviet system as such. In 1965, trials were held of people accused of "anti-Soviet agitation and propaganda." These were followed by the persecution of human rights activists who insisted on the authorities' honoring the Soviet constitution; the dispatching of some dissenters to mental health clinics; and moves against religious activists, nationalists, and so on. The physicist Andrei Sakharov, the father of the Soviet hydrogen bomb and latterly a dissident, was sent into internal exile; Solzhenitsyn was exiled abroad; while many others, like the famous cellist Mstislav Rostropovich, chose to leave.

In economic terms, Brezhnev's first decade was the best period in the history of the Soviet Union. The economy was growing fast, with new oil and gas fields as well as high dams and auto works coming on line, and so was popular consumption. For the first time, ordinary Soviet citizens could afford to buy cars; many were able to save and purchase better apartments; and high-quality foreign goods became available at the shops. In 1965, a modest attempt was made to reform the Soviet economy by introducing an element of profitability into it. This attempt, supported by Kosygin, however, failed to make the conomy more market-conscious and by the 1970s the reform was essentially abandoned. Yet life was fast improving. Health and education, science and technology made much progress. The Soviet Union's resources looked infinite, people's enthusiasm was great, and the demands on the system, albeit rising, were still modest. The Soviet welfare state was a reality.

Despite the tightening of the screws, and emigration of a number of key figures, Russian culture experienced nothing short of an explosion. Trailblazer Yuri Lyubimov's Taganka Theater became a mecca for the Moscow intelligentsia. Uncensored ballads sung by the poets Vladimir Vysotsky and Bulat Okudzhava were heard everywhere across the country. Films by Sergei Bondarchuk, Eldar Ryazanov, and Leonid Gaidai became classics of Russian cinematography. The intellectual debate between Sakharov and Solzhenitsyn stimulated free thinking along the lines of a convergence between socialism and capitalism, which was Sakharov's thesis, and the more conservative Russian patriotism defended by Solzhenitsyn. The religious thinker Alexander Men became a popular Orthodox preacher and writer. The party's arch-conservative ideologue, Mikhail Suslov, could still police and discipline the official sphere, but was powerless beyond it. This was the time of doublethink. Most people grew accustomed to saying directly opposite things in public and in private, never mixing their script.

From Confrontation to Détente to New Confrontation

Globally, the Soviet Union emerged as a superpower alongside the United States. The Cold War continued, but, after the Cuban missile crisis, certain rules were established. From the late 1960s, strategic arms limitation talks (SALT) became the heart of the US–Soviet relationship. The two countries also agreed, in the 1968 Non-Proliferation Treaty, to jointly prevent the emergence of new nuclear weapons states. After US President Richard Nixon's visit to Moscow in 1972, summits between US and Soviet leaders became regular events. Détente also involved European countries. Charles de Gaulle's vision of "Europe from the Atlantic to the Urals" and Willi Brandt's *Ostpolitik*, aimed at West Germany's reconciliation with the Soviet Union and its Eastern European allies, allowed the normalization of relations in the center of the continent. This culminated in the 1975 Helsinki Final Act, which recognized the post-war political set-up in Europe; promoted economic ties across the Cold War divide; and allowed humanitarian cooperation.

Détente, however, soon began to falter as the Soviet Union, buoyed in 1975 by the US defeat in Vietnam, pressed ahead with geopolitical advances in Africa, and the United States, under President Jimmy Carter, held up defense of human rights as a centerpiece of US foreign policy. The 1979 meeting between Brezhnev and Carter in Vienna, to sign the SALT-2 treaty, marked the end of détente. The treaty was never ratified. Later that same year, NATO passed a decision to deploy US medium-range missiles in Europe to counter the new Soviet systems, and the Soviet army invaded Afghanistan. In response, Washington imposed economic sanctions on the USSR and boycotted the 1980 Moscow Olympics. The USSR would respond four year later by shunning the Los Angeles Olympics.

By that time, the Soviet Union's international position was being challenged from a number of directions. First, relations with China were openly hostile and had worsened to the point of major border incidents in 1969 and 1973, with the USSR considering launching a nuclear attack against the People's Republic. Second, the Soviet bloc, after the 1968 Moscow-led Warsaw Pact intervention in Czechoslovakia, was again getting restive with the rise of the workers' Solidarity movement in Poland. And, third, Afghanistan turned out to be anything but a stabilization exercise. The Soviet military had to deal there with local fighters who were supported by the bulk of the ordinary people and assisted in many ways by the United States, its NATO allies, Pakistan, China, and the Arab countries. It is in Afghanistan where modern jihadism would be born.

Soviet Crisis

Challenged abroad, internally the Soviet Union had lost the last elements of its former dynamism. The economy slumped into stagnation. It was still technically growing – just – but its quantitative growth was often meaningless. Bureaucratic immobility and mismanagement played a role, as did the runaway militarization of the economy and the failure to use the benefits of technological progress in the civilian sector. Owing to the lack of either competition or profit, there were few stimuli to improve quality or the technological level of production. Agriculture, despite massive investment, remained a black hole. Ideology ruled, and inertia prevailed. The Soviet social state guaranteed full employment and a steady income. Between 1970 and 1985, those incomes, while still modest by Western standards, doubled – with little or no distinction being made between the best and worst workers. People's aspirations, however, were growing even faster in a country whose population, from 1945, had increased by about 100 million people.

The Soviet Union's erstwhile autarky was no more. Whereas Khrushchev, *in extremis*, had to sell one-third of the country's gold reserves to buy grain, Brezhnev proclaimed a "food program" but was regularly selling oil for food. The country became vulnerable to the fluctuations of the global market – which was particularly dangerous as it was living beyond its means. Brezhnev's physical decline, which first became visible in 1975, was emblematic of the country's deteriorating condition. He wanted to step down, but was persuaded to stay by the sycophants who sought to keep their own positions next to the nominal figure of the general secretary. No one moved, and nothing moved. The Politburo's gerontocracy became the laughing stock of the country and the world, but the Soviets were laughing with tears in their eyes.

When Brezhnev died in 1982, he was succeeded by Yuri Andropov, who for 15 years had headed the KGB.

At 68, this obviously intelligent man was already very ill. He was to die 15 months later. As he ascended to the top position in the USSR, Andropov memorably proclaimed that the leadership did not know the country in which it lived.[1] All his knowledge amassed while chairman of the KGB did not suffice to understand the dynamics of evolving Soviet society. Communist theory did not help much as a guide either. As a practical matter, Andropov sought to tighten the screws in a country where discipline had become very lax, and to pursue some of the corrupt officials of Brezhnev's former entourage. He did not achieve much in either direction.

Andropov's brief tenure was also notable for the low point in relations with the West. In 1983, the Soviet Union shot down a South Korean passenger plane that had strayed into Soviet airspace, killing over 200 people on board. Later the same year, the stalled US–Soviet nuclear arms talks were broken off and the United States began deploying Pershing II missiles in Europe with a short flying time to Moscow. Against the background of what was dubbed "the Euromissile crisis," senior Soviet military and security officials feared that a surprise decapitating US nuclear strike was imminent. After the Cuban missile crisis, this was perhaps the scariest moment in the history of the Cold War.

Andropov's successor in February 1984, Konstantin Chernenko, was Brezhnev's former personal assistant and lacked any stature in the party or the country.

He, like Andropov, was also ill from the very beginning and lasted barely a year. In 1985, with three state
funerals in Red Square in less than three years, the
Soviet Union faced its first-ever general crisis: political, economic, social, and spiritual. It was by no
means doomed, but it required a leader who could act
decisively, albeit thoughtfully, professionally, and very
carefully. What it got instead was a dreamer.

From Rehabilitation to Stagnation

The three decades that elapsed between Stalin's death
and the start of Mikhail Gorbachev's perestroika saw
the Soviet system mature and switch to a more peaceful mode of existence. There was much more freedom
than in the Stalinist period; there was peace inside the
country and – despite the Cold War – in its relations
with the outside world. In other words, the enormous
pressure of the preceding four decades dramatically
eased. The Soviet people entered a period of post-
traumatic rehabilitation. The Soviet system, however,
had proven itself far less capable of meeting the challenges of peacetime than those of upheaval.

Above all else, the legitimacy of the system was in
question. Faith in the Communist ideology and the
ideals of the 1917 revolution was wearing thin. A
tame attempt at economic reform was nipped in the
bud. The party elite, no longer expecting demotion
and death at the dictator's will, grew lazy, complacent,
and corrupt. Mass repression and widespread fear,

which had held ordinary people in check for decades in Stalin's time, decreased palpably. With the official values of the "builders of Communism's moral code" discredited, and traditional values seriously eroded in the post-revolutionary period, many people lacked any moral compass. The result was social demobilization and a general lack of direction. Most people agreed that the country had run into an impasse. Most hoped for a positive change led by a new kind of leadership: more open, bold, and forward-looking. Virtually no one, however, had the slightest idea of what sort of changes were about to happen, and how they would impact on everyone's life.

5

Democratic Upheaval (1985–99)

Mikhail Gorbachev, at 54 the youngest member of the
Politburo in March 1985, was a consensus candidate
to become the new general secretary. Ironically, his
selection by the Politburo put an end to consensus
decision-making in the Soviet Union. The best-
educated top Soviet leader since Lenin, Gorbachev had
been Andropov's protégé and Chernenko's effective
deputy. Now at the pinnacle of power, he meant to
become the supreme leader in practice as well as in
principle. Gorbachev was resolved to "do something"
to deal with the crisis of the Soviet system. He wanted
to rebuild the system that he now presided over.
He chose perestroika (rebuilding) as a short-hand
description of his course. The ambitious new leader,
however, had no clear image of the renewed system
that he was aspiring to, no plan for how to bring it
about, and, as it turned out, insufficient understanding of the country that he had inherited. Gorbachev's
early attempt to stamp out alcoholism by imposing
administrative restrictions and cutting production
spoke volumes about the level of his understanding.
Andropov's warning about the ignorance of those in
power should have been taken more seriously.

Perestroika and Glasnost

Gorbachev's early political slogan proclaimed "More socialism!" He sought to accelerate the moribund Soviet economy by relying on the "advantages of socialism," such as free education and health care, soon augmenting them with elements of the market, a kind of a new NEP, which he described not as the temporary tactical retreat that it was but as a new "late-Leninist" model to follow in the future. Gorbachev's "acceleration" of the existing system, however, was at cross-purposes with his own proclaimed need for reform. In 1986 at Chernobyl in Ukraine, as the result of human error, a nuclear powerplant exploded and contaminated a vast area, mostly in neighboring Belarus and parts of the Russian republic. Chernobyl, however, also laid bare numerous flaws in the Communist system: not just poor oversight and administrative sclerosis, but pervasive, even pathological, secrecy and utter disregard for human health and even life. Chernobyl symbolically diagnosed the state of Soviet governance.

Faced with growing obstacles to his reformist drive, which he ascribed to bureaucratic inertia, Gorbachev decided to appeal to ordinary people directly, stimulating and exploiting what he called "creativity of the masses." In parallel, he began to cleanse the Politburo, Central Committee, and regional party bodies of holdovers of the Brezhnev era, which he branded as one of *zastoi* (stagnation), and fill them with his own younger and more energetic appointees.

From 1987, Gorbachev began to accelerate his own policies. The new slogan was "More democracy!" By progressively removing more and more barriers to public criticism, and promoting glasnost (public debate), the young, dynamic, and instantly popular leader hoped to overcome the resistance of the party cadres. Gorbachev quickly became a hero for the Soviet intelligentsia. He freed political prisoners, who by the mid-1980s numbered about 1,000. Andrei Sakharov was allowed to return to Moscow from his internal exile in Gorky. Censorship was loosened. Literary ("thick") journals, political weeklies, and free "informal" newspapers captivated people's minds. Formerly banned books were published, including Solzhenitsyn's *Gulag Archipelago*. By 1990, censorship would finally be lifted. Lenin and the Communist Party were criticized alongside Stalin. In opening up the floodgates of political criticism, Gorbachev had come to rely on his ideology chief, Alexander Yakovlev, a former Soviet ambassador to Canada, who later admitted he had set out to destroy Soviet Communist ideology.

Freer speech was conquering ever more ground. Films like *Repentance* (1984) by Tenghiz Abuladze and *A Russia That We Lost* (1992) by Stanislav Govorukhin made people think about ethical issues in a totalitarian society and the price of Communist transformation. Radio jamming of foreign broadcasters was stopped, and the BBC Russian Service, Radio Liberty, and the Voice of America were allowed to broadcast without impediment. Soviet television itself showed unscripted debate on the screen – and live. Non-governmental organizations proliferated, from the liberal Memorial to the nationalist Pamyat, while countless political clubs and economic seminars attracted the more active part of the population. After the Soviet state agreed in 1988 to officially celebrate the millennium of Christianity's arrival in Russia, the Orthodox Church was increasingly liberated from state control. In 1990, a law on the freedom of conscience was passed. Those who wanted to leave the Soviet Union to live abroad were allowed out. Many decided to use what they thought was an always-ready-to-close window of opportunity. In 1987, emigration stood at 40,000; the next year, it almost tripled; in 1989, 235,000 Soviet citizens left for good; in 1990, the number reached 450,000.

Yet all these developments did little to improve the economic situation. The law on state enterprise proclaimed economic freedom and competition. However, the Soviet leadership would not face up to its inevitable consequences, such as unemployment as a result of factory closures, and higher prices. Soviet society was looking for instant improvements, not some hard slog. The reform stalled. What did work was private entrepreneurship, cooperatives, and occasional joint ventures with foreigners, which later became the nucleus of a new economy. Active people prepared to take risks and cut corners were in the ascendancy. The Soviet economy, by contrast, was in a tail spin. Dangerously, staple food items were becoming scarce even in the major cities.

Political Reform

It was then that Gorbachev first met a challenge not from the side of the conservative *nomenklatura*, but from the radicals and populists both within and outside the Communist Party. In 1987, Boris Yeltsin, then the Moscow party chief, publicly disagreed with the general secretary on the pace of perestroika – he wanted faster changes – and was demoted. To strengthen his position, in 1988 Gorbachev launched a political reform that aimed at shifting power from the party committees, which were still largely filled with conservatives, to the system of soviets, which combined the prerogatives of legislative and executive authority at all levels, from the township to the national parliament. Crucially, elections were to be competitive. This was a major step toward democracy and the rule of law. Politically, Gorbachev hoped his popularity would help him outflank the party.

The first ever partially free elections to the new Congress of People's Deputies held in the spring of 1989 produced unexpected results. In major cities, such as Moscow, Leningrad, and Sverdlovsk (now Yekaterinburg), local party bosses, whether appointed by Brezhnev or by Gorbachev himself, found it hard to get themselves elected. By contrast, a number of radical reformers got through. These included Sakharov and Yeltsin as well as the historian Yuri Afanasiev, the lawyer Anatoly Sobchak, and the economist Gavriil Popov. They formed a faction that demanded abolition of Article 6 of the Soviet constitution, which invested the Communist Party with the role of a "guiding and leading force" of Soviet society. The extremely candid proceedings of the two-week-long session of the Congress were broadcast live. Millions of people were transfixed by the televised debate, and then spent the rest of the day discussing the proceedings among themselves.

As the economic situation continued to worsen, social and political activity sharply increased. From the summer of 1989, miners started going on strike, blocking roads and railways. The Supreme Soviet, elected by the Congress, became the first Soviet leg-islature in permanent session. Gorbachev promul-gated the establishment of the first ever presidency of the Soviet Union and was elected to this new position – with 60% of the vote – by the Congress in March 1990. The radical opposition formed a bloc, Democratic Russia, which won a number of seats in the 1990 elections to the parliament of the Russian republic. A "democratic platform" emerged within the Communist Party. Conservatives responded by founding a Russian Communist Party, still within the CPSU. Non-communist parties were founded for the first time since the revolution.

The Rise of Nationalism

Reformist tendencies in the national capital sent tremors across the Soviet Union. With the party in disarray, and its repressive organs disoriented, turmoil was quick to follow. "Popular fronts for democracy" emerged in a number of republics. Ethnic conflicts erupted between the Armenians and the Azeris in Nagorno-Karabakh and the Abkhaz and the Georgians in Abkhazia. In the Baltic republics there were calls for restoration of their sovereignty, which had been snuffed out in 1940. Moldova was split down the Dniester River on the language issue. The death knell for the Soviet Union, however, was sounded in Moscow in June 1990, as the Russian republic's Supreme Soviet voted for Russia's state sovereignty. The empire would have withstood the challenges from the provinces: it might have released some from its grip, while suppressing or cajoling the others. It could do nothing, however, against the center that would not hold. Russians had had enough of the Soviet Union.

There is a temptation to explain Russia bolting out of the USSR as part of a power struggle between the Kremlin and the second echelon of the Soviet elite who held sway in the Russian Supreme Soviet. This is true, but only partly so. Since the 1970s, the Soviet Russian elites had been increasingly unhappy with the deal that Russia had within the USSR. Since the revolution, its resources had been used to develop the borderland republics and placate their elites and populations. Russia was giving so much more to the union than it was getting back. The other republics meanwhile were developing into increasingly ethnocratic polities. Seeing no future for them in the borderlands, ethnic Russians began to return to the Russian republic. The idea in 1990 was not to destroy the Soviet Union, but to get a proper compensation from the "sister republics." The Russian decision, however, touched off an avalanche of similar proclamations from the others. Those others, of course, believed that it was Russia that was ripping them off. The so-called "parade of sovereignties" was soon in full swing.

Gorbachev Is Overtaken by Events

One source of Gorbachev's tragedy was his reliance on the liberal intelligentsia and democratic circles. Initially, they helped him discredit the Stalinist state that he was trying to rebuild. Yet in their constant demand for ever more freedom they continued to push the reformist leader further than he believed it was safe for him – or the country – to go. Deserted by many of his supporters, who had moved on to support his arch-rival Boris Yeltsin, Gorbachev had no choice but to turn to the *nomenklatura*, whom he had been hitting hard. He pretended to be a "centrist," but his "center" had shrunk essentially to himself.

Gorbachev realized that things were getting out of control and made a last-ditch effort to reassert authority. In late 1990, he broke off relations with Yeltsin, saw one close associate, foreign minister Eduard Shevardnadze, resign, and another, the ideologue Alexander Yakovlev, called the *eminence grise* of glasnost, distance himself from him. Gorbachev appointed a mostly conservative cabinet. In January 1991, Soviet security services and the military used force to disperse demonstrators in Vilnius. Thirteen people died. In March, a referendum was held on the future of the Soviet Union. With the three Baltic republics, Georgia, Armenia, and Moldova, refusing to participate, about 75% of the voters supported a "reformed Soviet Union." Gorbachev began protracted negotiations on a new Union treaty. His effort was destined to fail. The time bomb planted in the Soviet constitution by Lenin and Stalin was ticking ever faster.

The Ultimate Détente

Despite the mounting difficulties at home, Gorbachev was lionized abroad, particularly in the West. In the late 1980s, Soviet foreign policy experienced a change no less dramatic than the country's political and economic scene. Initially, Gorbachev sought to lower the burden of the Soviet–American arms race and extricate the Soviet Union from the wolf's trap of Afghanistan. In one of his first government appointments, he replaced long-serving foreign minister Andrei Gromyko with a complete novice in the field, Eduard Shevardnadze, the Georgian party chief. Soon,

Gromyko's conservative style gave way to an exuberant new foreign policy ideology of sorts, which was called "new political thinking." Key to this ideology was the supremacy of universal values – such as the life and well-being of people – over class and national interests. It logically followed that in the present-day world, security could only be a common enterprise. Nuclear weapons stood in the way and had to be abolished by mutual consent of the superpowers.

The 1986 Reykjavik summit with US President Ronald Reagan was a turning point in nuclear disarmament. Already in 1987, the Soviet Union and the United States agreed to ban and destroy a whole class of weapons: intermediate-range ballistic missiles. In 1988, Gorbachev unilaterally renounced the use of force, and pledged to substantially reduce the Soviet military presence in Eastern Europe. In mid-1989, he advanced the idea of a common European home to which the USSR also belonged. All this reduced tensions and provided a more favorable international environment for the reforming Soviet Union.

Soon, however, the Soviet strategic position dramatically changed. In the fall of 1989, Gorbachev chose not to intervene as the Eastern European satellites, one by one, overthrew their Communist regimes, and the Berlin Wall opened. The loss of East Germany was a major blow to the entire Soviet strategic posture. However, Gorbachev saw this in terms of an historic reconciliation with the West. As he met with US President George H.W. Bush off Malta in December

1989, they declared the Cold War over. In 1990, Gorbachev agreed to a reunification of Germany by means of the Federal Republic absorbing the GDR and staying within NATO. Soviet forces in Germany, long the principal element of Moscow's position in Europe, were to leave within four years.

The Soviet Union was withdrawing also from other parts of the world. In February 1989, the decade-long Soviet war in Afghanistan, in which the USSR lost 13,833 servicemen,[1] ended with a negotiated settlement and the Soviet troops' pull-out. In May, Gorbachev traveled to China to meet with Deng Xiaoping and bury the hatchet of the Sino-Soviet confrontation. As part of the deal, after withdrawing from Afghanistan, the Soviet Union agreed to a with-drawal of its ally Vietnam's troops from Cambodia. Moscow was busy dialing back its presence around the world, from Africa (Angola, Mozambique, Namibia) to Central America (Nicaragua). In 1990, as the Soviet Union joined the United States in con-demning Saddam Hussein's invasion of Kuwait, and then allowed Washington to crush its nominal ally in Baghdad, Soviet influence in the Middle East was effectively over for a quarter of a century. The empire was gone.

The Fall of Communism and the End of the Soviet Union

In the summer of 1991, the Russian republic elected its own first president, Boris Yeltsin, who made no secret of his desire to place Russia, i.e. himself, above the Union, i.e. Gorbachev. At that time, Gorbachev was finalizing negotiations of the new Union treaty, which would have turned the USSR into a confederation with a sufficiently strong center. This was too much for more conservative forces in the Soviet leadership. In August 1991, on the eve of the treaty's signature, a group of senior officials, including the vice president, the newly appointed prime minister, ministers of the interior and defense, and the head of the KGB, proclaimed Gorbachev, who was vacationing in Crimea, temporarily incapacitated, and took over as a State of Emergency Committee.

The desperate attempt to save the Soviet Union fizzled out within three days. Yeltsin, who emerged as the leader of the resistance, triumphed. When Gorbachev was brought back from Crimea, Yeltsin made him publicly sign a decree banning the Communist Party. Gorbachev promptly resigned as the general secretary. The party was over. With the party gone, the Soviet Union inevitably started to unravel. In September, Estonia, Latvia, and Lithuania were formally allowed to secede from the USSR. In November, Yeltsin announced that Russia would carry out economic reforms on its own.

On December 1, 1991, 84% of Ukrainians voted to form an independent state – against 70% who had supported a reformed Soviet Union just a few months earlier. On December 8, the leaders of Russia, Ukraine, and Belarus met in a Belarusian hunting lodge to formally dismantle the Soviet Union, which they had established in 1922. They also agreed to form a Commonwealth of Independent States – a loose association of the former Soviet republics. Over time, the CIS, with its hundreds of non-performing agreements, would prove to be a successful vehicle not for reintegration but just the opposite: the gradual undoing of the many bonds that linked the imperial borderlands-turned-Soviet republics.

On December 25, 1991, Mikhail Gorbachev, during a televised address to the nation, resigned as president. The Soviet flag atop the Kremlin was replaced with the Russian tricolor. When Gorbachev ascended to the top position, the Soviet Union was experiencing its first comprehensive crisis: economic, societal, ideological, and spiritual. He tried to deal with it by loosening controls and encouraging initiative, but in the end he only managed to achieve a soft landing for the system that he had set out to reform. Although Gorbachev appeared the obvious leadership choice in 1985, other possibilities existed. A different leader would have certainly taken the country in a different direction. Deng Xiaoping's example of reforming the economy while keeping tight control of politics already stood before the eyes of the Soviet leadership.

Gorbachev's main problem was loss of control, the ultimate blunder for any Russian leader.

In 1991, most Russian people did not mourn the end of the Communist system. They hoped that the advent of a new Russia would be a new beginning marked by freedom, prosperity, and amicable relations with the rest of the world. Many rejected the Soviet period outright as a time when "we were in a permanent war with ourselves," as popular singer Viktor Tsoi put it. The new Russia, people hoped, was going to redeem the oppression, un-freedom, and misery of the Soviet Union. Unlike in 1917, however, there was no bitterness, no desire to settle scores. The degree of tolerance was unprecedented.

Economic Reforms

As Gorbachev moved out, Yeltsin moved in. The Russian Federation immediately recognized all former republics as sovereign states in their Soviet-era borders – even though some 25 million ethnic Russians ended up on the wrong side of those borders.

For the new leadership in the Kremlin, economic reforms were the top priority. In January 1992, Yegor Gaidar, the 34-year-old acting prime minister appointed by Yeltsin, announced liberalization of domestic and foreign trade, abolition of price controls, and wholesale privatization. Reforms were immediately placed on a fast track, and the more gradualist Eastern European path to the market was rejected:

Gaidar and his colleagues feared a Communist come-back. This approach pushed most Russian people into a survival mode, while offering rapid enrichment to a few. Privatization was seen as a sham – *prikhvatization* – which meant a cover for stealing. Those with access to senior government officials benefited from such mechanisms as import subsidies, industrial soft cred-its, and low domestic energy and metals prices, which made exporting them so lucrative. The latter was later described as "access to the pipeline." Government officials routinely got a percentage of the deals they approved. This is how early fortunes were made.

Those who had nothing better to do but to try to survive were kept afloat by informal employment and small private plots of land where they could grow vegetables. Officially, unemployment was low – 12% maximum – but salaries, in any event very small, were paid most irregularly. Ditto for pensions. By 1999, 40% of the population were officially categorized as poor. The degree of inequality shot up.[2] Money was scarce; barter trade became ubiquitous. Many people had to sell their belongings; others became shuttle traders, traveling to places like Poland, Turkey, and China to bring back goods to sell in Russia, or invested in Ponzi schemes popularly called "pyramids." Inflation was rife, reaching 2,500% in 1992. Living standards plummeted; the former Soviet middle class was wiped out, along with most people's savings. To some, Russia looked finished.

Meanwhile, privatization of the Russian economy

proceeded rapidly. Anatoly Chubais, who directed it, was busy creating a class of property owners who would prevent a Communist return to power. By 1994, already over 50% of the economy was in private hands; by 1995, this reached 58%, and by 2000, 62%. The government was short of money, and it staged "loans for shares" auctions, in which it gave away major enterprises for a fraction of their real value. Thus, Norilsk Nickel went for $170 million (its value in 2001 was $10 billion); Yukos for $350 million ($9 billion in 1997); Sibneft, for just $100 million.[3] Loans were never repaid, and the property remained in private hands. This is how large chunks of the Russian economy happened to become the property of a few individuals, who came to be known as the "oligarchs": Roman Abramovich, Vagit Alekperov, Boris Berezovsky, Vladimir Gusinsky, Vladimir Potanin, and several others, including members of President Yeltsin's family.

The results of these efforts were spectacular. On the positive side, there was suddenly a market in place; as if by a miracle, goods and services became abundant. Commerce and banking business boomed. Russia was being fast integrated into the global economy. However, investing in Russia was risky owing to the political uncertainty and the high level of crime. The Russian economy badly needed investment, but money was leaving the country at an annual rate of $15–20 billion – compare this with the total of $27 billion that Russia received in the 1990s from the International

Monetary Fund and the World Bank. The Soviet-era economy rapidly disintegrated. The GDP was down by 40%. Science and technology, health, education, and culture rapidly degraded. Births became rare, but deaths skyrocketed. Life expectancy for men plunged from 64 in 1990 to 57 in 1995.

Political Crisis and a New Constitution

As the Soviet Union was formally dismantled, the Russian Federation, within the borders of the Soviet Russian republic, continued to function as the continuation state of the USSR. Soviet laws continued to operate, except where they were superseded by new ones. The Soviet Russian constitution, though heavily amended, was still in force. President Yeltsin and the Congress of People's Deputies, alongside its Supreme Soviet, elected in 1991 and 1990, respectively, remained in place. The Communist Party, banned in August 1991, was revived – as an opposition force – as early as 1992. The Soviet military forces in the Russian territory and outside the former USSR came under Russian jurisdiction. The military high command pledged loyalty to Yeltsin already in November 1991, which ensured that the Soviet Union would have a soft rather than a hard landing. The state security apparatus was reformed, but not disbanded. Thus, politically there was no radical break with the past, which helped avoid a new civil war in Russia.

Yet it did not prevent a confrontation between the

president and his radical reformist team, on the one hand, and the Supreme Soviet, on the other. In late 1992, the parliament insisted on Gaidar's departure from the government. He was replaced as prime minister by Viktor Chernomyrdin, a top manager from the gas industry. The existing constitution did not make it clear which of the two – the president or parliament – wielded supreme authority in the land. In April 1993, Yeltsin won a vote of confidence in a national referendum, but the stand-off continued. When in September the president moved to dissolve the Supreme Soviet, the latter refused and holed up in the parliament building – the one that was Yeltsin's headquarters in August 1991. The Supreme Soviet, led by its speaker, Ruslan Khasbulatov, declared the president dismissed and formed its own government. Vice President Alexander Rutskoi, who had broken with Yeltsin and joined with the Supreme Soviet, was proclaimed the new leader. On October 3–4, 1993, a "little civil war" occurred in the center of Moscow. As Supreme Soviet supporters tried to storm the TV station and called for a march on the Kremlin, Yeltsin ordered the military to put down resistance. The parliament building was shelled. The deputies surrendered. Yeltsin triumphed. The official death toll stood at 146, but unofficial reports put it much higher.

In December 1993, a new constitution was adopted in a referendum. This constitution, in force to this day, was squarely based on democratic principles, the rule of law, and respect for human rights. It established the Russian Federation as a presidential republic with a strong bi-cameral parliament (the State Duma and the Federation Council) and an independent judiciary complete with a Constitutional Court. The country's many regions received substantial rights. The authors of the document evidently took their inspiration from the American and French constitutions. For the Russia of the 1990s, however, the new basic law was more of a model to grow into than a description of the existing realities.

The Political System of Yeltsin's Russia

The constitutional referendum was accompanied by the first elections to the State Duma. To the consternation of many liberals, mesmerized by new post-Communist freedoms and less concerned with the economic sufferings of many voters, the reformers of Russia's Democratic Choice did rather badly. The nationalists, misnamed liberal democrats and led by Vladimir Zhirinovsky, finished first among the party lists. The Communists, headed by Gennady Zyuganov, also won a strong representation. The first Duma continuously challenged the government and the president, who, lacking a majority, had to put up with compromise decisions. The next election held in 1995 did not alter the situation too much. The Duma established itself as the bulwark of the left- and nationalist-leaning opposition.

The crucial test was the 1996 presidential elections.

Yeltsin's popularity sank to single digits <u>and</u> there was a good chance that the next president would be the Communist Zyuganov. Fears were running high of a Communist backlash, which caused the oligarchs the most concern. In early 1996, at a meeting on the margins of the World Economic Forum in Davos, Chubais and the seven top tycoons (the "seven bankers") formed an alliance to get Yeltsin re-elected. They managed to mobilize all financial, political, and media resources at hand, and reached out to American campaign managers. In the first ballot, Yeltsin just got ahead of Zyuganov (35% vs. 32%), but in the second one he carried the day (54% vs. 41%). Democracy and the oligarchs were saved.

The Chechen War

While civil war in Russia was being avoided, a different war was raging. In 1991, as the Soviet Union was falling apart, a number of territories below the level of Soviet constituent republics – Nagorno-Karabakh in Azerbaijan, Abkhazia and South Ossetia in Georgia – declared their sovereignty, which led to conflict. In the North Caucasus, Chechnya proclaimed its independence in September 1991. For three years, the separatist regime led by a former Soviet general, Dzhokhar Dudayev, was basically tolerated by Moscow, which had too much on its plate. Once the crisis in the capital was over, however, the Russian leadership turned its attention to the rebellious province. In December

1994, Yeltsin ordered restoration of the constitutional order in Chechnya, thus sparking the war.

The badly led and poorly equipped Russian army found it hard to fight a campaign both in the urban environment of Grozny, Chechnya's capital, and in the mountainous areas. The war became almost immediately unpopular with the bulk of the population. The Russian army, like the Soviet one, was a conscript force, and the war in Chechnya looked to most like a sequel to another recent senseless and bloody engagement – in Afghanistan. Russian officers and men fought – and many died – for the country's unity even as the politicians in Moscow used the war for maximizing their power and profit. The Russian liberal-dominated media mostly sided with the Chechens against the Russian army. Russian human rights campaigners accused the military of war crimes. Yet, by mid-1995, Russia was prevailing.

It was at that time that the Chechen separatists reversed the tide of the war. In 1995 and again in early 1996, they carried out terrorist raids deep inside adjacent Russian regions and took a thousand hostages each time. Taken by surprise, the leaders in Moscow decided to capitulate to save innocent civilians. This boosted the rebels' morale and disoriented the Russian military. In May 1996, in the final stages of his presidential campaign, Yeltsin invited a Chechen separatist delegation to the Kremlin. A truce was signed and Russian forces withdrew from the region. Yet the problem was not solved. Within Chechnya, Islamist radicals defeated secular separatists. Southern Russian regions were again subjected to kidnappings, looting, and terrorist raids from across the administrative border.

Chechnya was an extreme, but not a unique, case of separatism in post-Soviet Russia. A number of other regions, some of them constituted as homelands of particular ethnic groups, others ethnically Russian, declared themselves sovereign, proclaimed their laws superior to those of the Russian Federation, and vowed to establish direct links with foreign countries. It appeared that Russia was going down the path of the Soviet Union. The potentially most dangerous case was not Chechnya, but Tatarstan, a sizeable republic on the Volga, right in the heart of Russia. Conflict was averted through the wisdom of the Tatar president, Mintimer Shaymiev, and of the Russian officials dealing with Tatarstan. Instead Moscow and Kazan, the Tatar capital, signed a special treaty governing their relations.

The Search for Yeltsin's Successor

Soon into his second mandate, Yeltsin's health began to fail. In November 1996, he had to undergo an open heart operation. As the president re-emerged in the Kremlin a few months later, a search for his successor was launched. Yeltsin and his family looked at different candidates: liberal reformers, technocrats, and security professionals. In March 1998, Yeltsin suddenly replaced Prime Minister Viktor Chernomyrdin, whom many regarded as an heir apparent. The new incumbent was a young liberal-leaning technocrat, Sergei Kiriyenko. His tenure turned out to be very short, but it was marked by a momentous development: a financial crisis.

Yeltsin's re-election instilled confidence in the Russian political system among potential investors. Russian government bonds grew popular, but the ruble soon became overvalued. The sudden fall in the oil price, to $13 a barrel, made it impossible for the government to service its debt. In August 1998, Russia defaulted on its obligations. The ruble fell four times against the US dollar. Inflation jumped to 96% in 1998, before slipping to a still substantial 36% in 1999. People's incomes, meanwhile, plunged by 250%. Yet this crisis helped relaunch the market and the Russian economy.

Pressed by the Duma, Yeltsin reluctantly agreed to appoint Foreign Minister Yevgeny Primakov head of the Russian government. Primakov's short-lived cabinet – he would be sacked by Yeltsin in May 1999 – managed the crisis well, but it fell foul of the president's jealousy. From the Yeltsin family's perspective, Primakov could not be trusted as a successor. They feared he would send them to jail, and looked at other candidates, until they found Vladimir Putin, head of the FSB (Federal Security Service, one of the successors to the KGB) and secretary of the national Security Council. The family correctly singled out Putin's central psychological feature: loyalty. Putin had stood by his mentor Sobchak when St. Petersburg's first mayor, having lost an election, got in trouble and he helped him flee abroad. In August 1999, Putin was appointed prime minister. The succession process was then set in motion.

Russia's Western Integration Fails

Russia's foreign policy in the 1990s was mainly pursuing two goals: integration into the Western system; and managing relations with the republics of the former Soviet Union. Integration did not work for a number of reasons. Russia was far bigger and thus more complex than any other former Communist country; its break with the past was far less radical and its economic, social, and political transformations lagged behind; and "returning to Europe/joining the West" was not the single focus of its elites and society, in contrast to virtually everywhere else in Eastern Europe. The most important factor, however, was the refusal of the Russian elites to drop their great power mentality and accept US global leadership.

Nevertheless, for a few years it looked as though an integration with the West was possible. Yeltsin's first foreign minister, Andrei Kozyrev, saw close ties to the West and particularly the United States as a sine qua non for Russia's democratic transformation. Yet as new capitalism was taking root in Russia, and Western support no longer seemed critical, this position was becoming untenable. US actions such as NATO's enlargement to Eastern Europe and military intervention in the Balkans, which ignored Moscow's protests, revealed serious geopolitical differences between Russia and its new partners. In 1996, Kozyrev was replaced by Primakov, now head of the Foreign Intelligence Service, who had a more realist attitude toward international relations. In March 1999, as the US-led NATO air war against Serbia over Kosovo was launched, Primakov was en route to Washington. He ordered his plane to reverse course and return to Russia. This was a symbolic end to the unique decade-long period of Russia's attempted integration into the West.

Closer to home, Moscow immediately recognized all former Soviet republics as independent states in their 1991 borders. Despite officially calling the CIS its foreign policy priority, Moscow put the relationships with the ex-provinces on a back burner. With US assistance, it secured transfer of all former Soviet strategic nuclear weapons from Ukraine, Belarus, and Kazakhstan to Russia. It used its military forces deployed in the areas of conflict in Abkhazia, South Ossetia, and Transnistria to freeze ethnic conflicts there and protect the breakaway territories. In Tajikistan, where the conflict was not ethnically rooted, it was actually settled politically, with Moscow teaming with Tehran to restore peace. While intra-CIS borders stayed open, Russia continued to subsidize its energy exports, particularly to Ukraine and Belarus.

Loss of Control Leads to Chaos

The 1990s were the longest freest period of virtually unrestricted political freedom in Russian history. The material situation was hard, the political, unsettled, but ideological tendencies and schools of thought flowered. Virtually everything that had ever been banned flourished. The arts, initially hit hard by the abrupt change in the economic situation, began to revive in the middle of the decade. Even more impressive was the revival of religion. Led by the Patriarch Alexy II, elected in 1990, the Russian Orthodox Church returned from the fringes of society right into its heart. Russians began to identify themselves with Orthodox Christianity, even if not all became actual believers after three-quarters of a century of official atheism.

Ten years after Gorbachev's celebration of baptism of Russia, the Kremlin – now under Yeltsin – took another step toward reconciliation with the country's past. In July 1998, 80 years after their murder near Yekaterinburg, the remains of Nicholas II and his family members, recovered from a mine shaft, were given a state funeral in St. Petersburg's Peter and Paul cathedral, alongside the other Russian emperors. This was a symbolic closing of books on the tragedy of the Russian revolution. Russia's twentieth-century history had come a full circle.

By the end of the last decade of the twentieth century, Russia was in a pathetic condition. The state had virtually ceased to exist; the oligarchy ruled. Law enforcement hardly functioned. The central government's budget depended on handouts from the International Monetary Fund. Regional barons paid little attention to the federal authorities. Chechen separatists seemed 10 feet tall, virtually invincible. The Russian Federation looked destined to repeat the path of the Soviet Union: that is, to disintegrate into separate entities. US experts were getting ready for a world without Russia, and foreign journalists in Moscow actively speculated where exactly the new fault lines would emerge. Some thought the military districts might be the only units capable of sustaining themselves. Rarely in its history had Russia appeared more pitiful. This was about to change.

6

From Stability to Uncertainty (2000–19)

In that darkest moment of September 1999, Chechen extremists led by Shamil Basayev, who had launched the 1995 raid, invaded the neighboring Russian republic of Dagestan in an effort to ignite an Islamist rebellion against Russian rule. In September, explosions in a number of apartment blocks in Moscow and Volgograd killed hundreds of people. Then, to the surprise of many, a pushback occurred. Putin, together with the chief of the General Staff, Anatoly Kvashnin, immediately organized a successful counter-terrorist operation in Dagestan and then took the fight to Chechnya itself. To Putin, Russia faced a mortal danger: originating in the North Caucasus, Islamist extremism and terrorism threatened other Muslim republics, such as Tatarstan, and could reach the Russian heartland. He vowed to stop the terrorists and annihilate them in their den.[1]

Putin Succeeds Yeltsin

The second campaign in Chechnya began just as Russia was preparing for a new Duma election, to be held in December 1999. This time the winners of 1996 were split. Primakov and Moscow mayor Yuri Luzhkov built a strong bloc that challenged the positions of the Kremlin group, centered on the Yeltsin family. The billionaire Boris Berezovsky, who as a deputy head of the National Security Council and executive secretary of the CIS was the ultimate oligarch, countered the Primakov–Luzhkov move with a project of his own, a coalition of liberal "statists" led by the well-regarded minister for emergency situations, Sergei Shoigu, and the increasingly popular prime minister, Vladimir Putin. This coalition, called "Unity," won big – in no small measure owing to Putin's bold response to the terrorist challenge. Less than two weeks later, in a televised address on New Year's Eve, 1999, Yeltsin stunned the nation by resigning and handing over to Putin as acting president. A new era began.

In March 2000, Putin won the presidential election with 53% of the vote. As Russia's top leader in the early twenty-first century, he had two main goals. The first was to keep Russia in one piece. The second was to restore Russia's status as a great power. Putin's immediate objective was to reinstate the authority of the Russian state, which had been seriously weakened in the upheavals of the previous decade. The first obstacle on that path were the oligarchs who had thought they would be able to manipulate the new president whom they had chosen as Yeltsin's successor, along with Yeltsin's family. Putin later disclosed that the oligarchs had warned him against asserting his independence. He ignored the warning. Within a few months, the Kremlin kingmaker Boris Berezovsky and the media mogul Vladimir Gusinsky lost their power, influence, and even (in Gusinsky's case) their freedom – if briefly. They both soon ended up in exile: Berezovsky in Britain, and Gusinsky in Israel.

In 2003, Putin faced a new challenge from another oligarch. Mikhail Khodorkovsky, the billionaire owner of Yukos oil company, was openly developing political ambitions, buying votes in the Duma, funding NGOs, and talking about removing Putin from power. He was also negotiating behind Putin's back to sell Yukos to ExxonMobil. These actions ran directly counter to the binary choice that the president had offered the oligarchs: you can do business or engage in politics, but you cannot do both. What was at stake was supreme power in the land, and Putin acted decisively to keep it to himself. Khodorkovsky was arrested, tried for tax fraud, jailed for 10 years, served almost the entire term, and released in 2013, ahead of the Sochi Olympics. Having settled abroad, he has been a virulent critic of Putin ever since.

The second obstacle were the regional barons – governors of regions and presidents of republics within Russia – who during the 1990s had grabbed much real power in their fiefdoms, which they sometimes ruled as their patrimony. Putin asserted the primacy of the federal constitution over regional legislation, and abolished the practice of the Federation cutting special deals with various regions. The country was divided into seven federal districts, as sort of governorships general, each overseen by a presidential envoy, who had authority over regional governors. The governors also lost their special status as members of the upper chamber of the federal parliament, and were offered instead a seat on the exclusively advisory body, the newly created Council of State, to be convened by the president as necessary.

The third obstacle was the State Duma, the lower house of parliament, which during Yeltsin's time was dominated by the opposition to the Kremlin. In 1999, it nearly impeached the president. In the 2003 elections, Putin-supported United Russia won two-thirds of the seats and dealt a major blow to the Communist Party, the main opposition force, whose representation in parliament was decisively reduced, never to recover. The democratic and liberal parties, Yabloko and the Union of Right Forces, failed to clear the 7% threshold and have been out of the Duma since then. The threshold and the new legislation which required that parties have at least 50,000 registered members also allowed the Kremlin to eliminate dozens of small political formations, which largely benefited United Russia.

Removal of these obstacles allowed the Kremlin to establish what Putin called a "dictatorship of law" and a "power vertical." With all branches of power under centralized control, and the party of power (United Russia) functioning as an election machine to give legitimacy to the political system, Putin carried out an administrative reform designed to streamline governance. In effect, what he did was to restore state bureaucracy as the bedrock of the state and the main instrument of wielding power in Russia. In the 2004 elections, Putin won 71% of the vote. Ascribing that victory solely to himself, he replaced the last hold-overs of the Yeltsin team, Prime Minister Mikhail Kasyanov and head of the Presidential Administration Alexander Voloshin, and was now fully sovereign.

Chechnya's Pacification

During his first term, Putin had to deal with the issue of terrorism, particularly as related to Chechnya. There, he also moved with full determination. In 2000, Grozny, the capital of Chechnya, was brought fully under the control of the federal forces. By 2002, major fighting in the mountains of Chechnya had stopped. Having ignored the advice of many to install a military governor to pacify the province, Putin had the insight of turning the Chechen administration over to the Chechens themselves. For the role of the head of the Chechen republic within Russia, Putin chose a mufti who during the first campaign in the mid-1990s had fought against the federal forces, Akhmat Kadyrov.

This proved to be an auspicious move. Within a few years, Chechnya, ruled by the Kadyrov clan with an iron fist and with the Kremlin's full backing, became pacified. With Moscow's financial aid, it was able to rebuild what had been damaged in the war, and essentially developed into a version of what the early separatists had dreamed about: a largely self-ruling and reasonably prosperous province with a minimal Russian presence, either civilian, police, or military; a leader of Islam within Russia; and a place with extensive ties to Muslim countries across the world. Even though Akhmat Kadyrov was assassinated in 2004, his son Ramzan soon took over and is now ruling Chechnya almost as a sovereign in a sort of a personal union with Putin.

While Chechnya itself was being increasingly rehabilitated, terrorism elsewhere in Russia remained an issue. In October 2002, about 800 people were held hostage at Moscow's Dubrovka Theater by an armed terrorist group. The storming of the building resulted in 140 hostages being killed by the gas used to disable the attackers. In September 2004, another terrorist gang took over a school in Beslan, North Ossetia. Again, the storming of the building by the security forces led to the deaths of many hostages, with over 300 people killed, most of them schoolchildren. Days before that attack happened, terrorists had blown up two passenger planes on domestic flights, leaving scores of people dead. These were heart-wrenching tragedies, which also pointed to the failure of the security services to prevent such raids and to deal with their consequences. Over time, they would learn the lessons to address the continuing threat of terrorism more effectively.

Stabilization of the Political Regime

Meanwhile, Putin evolved from, as he himself put it in 2002, a "hired manager" of the country to someone more like a modern tsar. By the mid-2000s, his personal rule was firmly established. The former oligarchs were reduced to being just very wealthy people entrusted by the Kremlin with the immense assets that they nominally controlled. Regional elites had to renounce the last vestiges of separatism and were all dependent on the federal government for financial and political support. The parliament became an extension of the Presidential Administration, and the opposition was partly domesticated (the Communists), partly marginalized (the liberals). Chechnya, against most predictions, was not only pacified but became a true ally of the Kremlin. The state's authority was re-established, and the government bureaucracy reasserted itself as the mainstay of the political and politico-economic systems.

The Yeltsin-era ruling elite was not wholly replaced, but it had to make room for new entrants. These came primarily from the security community of the KGB/FSB (Federal Security Service), and also included a number of the president's personal friends and acquaintances from his years of service in East Germany and Leningrad/St. Petersburg. These very different people – Igor Sechin (Rosneft), Alexei Miller (Gazprom), Sergei Chemezov (Rostech), Gennady Timchenko (Volga Group), Mikhail and Yury Kovalchuk (Kurchatov Institute), Yury Kovalchuk (Rossiya Bank), Sergei Shoigu (defense minister), Nikolai Patrushev (Security Council secretary and former director of the FSB), and Herman Gref

(Sberbank) – became the most influential members of the Putin elite. Their predecessors, from Roman Abramovich to Anatoly Chubais, Yuri Luzhkov, and Yeltsin's family members, retained their wealth or status, but had to accept a considerable reduction of their influence. In Russia, power and influence are a function not of wealth but rather of the proximity to the throne.

Putin's power rests not only on his firm control of the elites, but also on the support that he gets from the bulk of average Russians, and the latter is more important. The secret of Putin's staying power at the top of the Russian system – remember: both Yeltsin and Gorbachev, very popular at the beginning, soon lost popularity and ended up badly – is his ability to reach out to millions of ordinary people, and to feel their needs. His humble background certainly helped, but there is something else. He may be one of the very few people in power in contemporary Russia credited with being genuinely interested in the country and caring for its people, not just busy enriching himself or indulging his personal vanity.

Economic Rehabilitation

Putin inherited an economy that was weak but quickly bouncing back from the default of 1998. He took economic issues seriously and was convinced that the real cause of the collapse of the Soviet Union was its unviable economic system. The first thing he did as acting president was to establish a Center for Strategic Research to come up with a blueprint for economic reform. In 2000–3, a number of reforms were carried out in such areas as taxation, land ownership, and public administration. From the mid-2000s, however, the reform effort stalled as rapidly rising oil prices meant that the Kremlin could throw money at problems and had less incentive to deal with their structural causes. Yet Moscow's macroeconomic and financial policies remained prudent. Windfall profits from oil and gas trade were not squandered, but put away in the Stabilization and National Welfare Funds. Inflation was brought down from 20% in 2000 to 9% in 2006.

The ownership structure of the Russian economy underwent major changes. Most important was the consolidation of the oil sector in government hands. The nationalization of the Yukos company and its takeover by state-owned Rosneft was the most salient move in this direction. As a result, the share of state ownership in the oil industry jumped from 13% in 2004 to 40% in 2007. Overall, state-owned companies, which accounted for 35% of GDP in 2005, doubled that share by 2015.[2] State capitalism replaced the oligarchical system as the most distinctive characteristic of contemporary Russian economy. Next to Gazprom and Rosneft, other state corporations emerged – e.g. United Energy Systems (later privatized), Transneft, Russian Railways, United Aircraft, and United Shipbuilding – as well as banks

– e.g. Sberbank, VTB, and VTB-24. The Kremlin also strengthened control of Russia's arms exports.

This tight nexus of power and money had the negative effect of fostering corruption and corroding exactly the departments of the government charged with decision-making, law enforcement, and judicial oversight. All too often, members of the new power elites acquired business interests of their own and used their position against competitors by means of raiding their businesses, framing them in court, and organizing hostile mergers. Corruption, according to a popular saying, has ceased to be a bug in the system – it became *the* system itself. This will perhaps be the most problematic part of the legacy of Vladimir Putin's reign.

Social Transformation

Ironically, while property holdings at the top and higher echelons proved to be less secure, at grassroots levels there was a gradual and grudging acceptance of private property. The legal system, despite all its imperfections and distortions, which were most visible at higher levels, began to work. Russia did not transform itself into a society of law-abiding citizens, of course, but recourse to the courts became routine. Oil-spurred economic growth allowed a sharp reduction in the poverty rate. Salaries and wages, but also pensions, grew substantially after 2000. Russia began to turn into a nation of consumers. A post-Soviet middle class was emerging, particularly in Moscow, St. Petersburg, Nizhny Novgorod, Rostov, Yekaterinburg, and other larger cities.

Yet this was also a society of high inequality. In 2005, Russia had 44 billionaires (Moscow counted more of them than New York City) and 90,000 millionaires.[3] There were very few outbursts against these people's wealth, however ill-gotten, but there was also a push-back against anything that looked like a termination of Soviet-era social benefits. When the government tried to replace some benefits in kind with monetary payments, there were suddenly spontaneous mass protests against the measure. The government had to make concessions. For a long time after that, the Kremlin desisted from anything that might endanger social peace, including a much-needed pension reform.

Another new feature to be internalized were regular elections. After the adoption of the current constitution in 1993, all Russian elections ran on schedule. Concerned by the fall-out from the so-called "color revolutions" in Georgia (2003), Kyrgyzstan (2005), and particularly Ukraine (2004), the Kremlin perfected its techniques of political manipulation that guaranteed desirable results in elections at different levels. Yet the principle of elections, however constrained in practice, was never abandoned. While the bulk of the Russian people did not aspire to changing power through elections, they got used to being periodically consulted by the powers-that-be about the elites' choice for various positions, from the president down. Like acceptance of the principle of private property – despite all the objections to how this was exercised in practice – the acceptance of elections as the only formal instrument for replacing people in high places, again, all the exceptions notwithstanding, has formed a major achievement of the Putin era.

Medvedev's Failed Modernization and Putin's Return to the Kremlin

The president led by example. In 2008, when his second term was running out, rather than changing the constitution, as most people around him and in the country at large expected and actually wanted, Putin chose to present a hand-picked successor, Dmitry Medvedev, and help him get elected. Putin himself became prime minister and, while not impinging on the formal prerogatives of the president, remained the most influential person in the country. The so-called "tandemocracy" lasted the entire four years of Medvedev's mandate, and was terminated when Putin had concluded that Russia's domestic situation and international position would be vulnerable if Medvedev were allowed a second term.

Domestically, economic development suffered as a result of the 2008–9 global financial crisis and the top leadership's unwillingness to break through structural logjams. With 43-year-old Medvedev in the Kremlin, modernization remained a buzz word, while the government focused on battling the crisis. The widely publicized national projects in health, education, communal services, and agriculture were only partially fulfilled. The growth of the middle class stalled. The Russian economy remained by and large a hostage of the fluctuating oil price.

Putin's decision, announced in September 2011, to run for presidency again, which was technically possible – the Russian constitution forbids only a third *consecutive* term – brought dismay among part of the elites who had banked on Medvedev, and the new young urban classes who had grown tired of Putin's long rule. Their dissatisfaction morphed into mass street protest after the December elections to the Duma, which were widely regarded as rigged in favor of the United Russia party. For months ahead of the presidential poll and Putin's eventual return to the Kremlin in May 2012, Bolotnaya Square across the river from the Kremlin became the venue for protesters' gatherings numbering over 120,000 – the highest number seen since the final years of the Soviet Union. Initially peaceful, these rallies turned violent on the eve of the presidential inauguration, which resulted in arrests, jail sentences, and new harsher legislation governing protest activities.

The Bolotnaya protests marked the failure of the policies that sought to moderate dissent by means of integrating dissenters into Kremlin-organized pseudo-political activity. The ideology of sovereign democracy promoted by Putin's domestic politics adviser,

Vladislav Surkov, in the wake of the color revolutions provided for a diversity of political views and societal orientations – on condition that they would all remain under the Kremlin's politico-technological control. The idea was that the Kremlin would not only organize the party of power; it would also organize and manage various forms of opposition to it. This simulation of politics, however, ultimately did not work.

Social and Cultural Scene

The new course that domestic politics took did not pretend to offer everything to everybody. Sovereign democracy was toned down, replaced by Russian patriotism. Since he came to power, Putin had been seeking to restore the unity of Russian history, which he saw as squarely centered on the Russian state – in all its incarnations. In 2000, in a grand compromise with the still powerful Communist Party, the Kremlin managed to have the tsarist double-headed eagle established as the official state emblem. Simultaneously, the Soviet-era national anthem was brought back as the anthem of the Russian Federation. The words had to be rewritten by the author of the original 1943 text, approved by Stalin, and who had done the rewriting once before, at Brezhnev's behest in 1977.

In the 2000s, the revival of the Russian Orthodox Church (ROC), begun under the leadership of Patriarch Alexy II in 1990, reached its peak. Symbolically, Our Savior's cathedral, a landmark building next to the

Kremlin that, as we saw in chapter 2, was blown up on Stalin's orders in 1931, was rebuilt in 2001. In 2007, the Moscow Patriarchate and the Russian Orthodox Church Abroad, split since the 1920s, agreed to come together again. President Putin played a major role in reunifying the two branches of the church separated by the Civil War. By 2006, the ROC numbered 27,500 parishes, compared to just 7,500 in 1960. Patriarch Kirill, who succeeded Alexy II in 2009, became a leading voice in debates on social and ethical issues, strengthening the conservative strain of domestic politics.

Instead of trying to co-opt the dissenters, the Kremlin moved to isolate the leaders of anti-government protest and pacify the rest by bringing the metropolitan centers of the country more in line with cities in Western Europe. The leaders of protests were jailed, like the Left Front's Sergei Udaltsov and a range of Bolotnaya protesters, or put under house arrest, like the anti-corruption activist Alexei Navalny. Incensed with Western financial support for many of the Russian NGOs that were critical of the state's policies, the Kremlin forced them either to accept the label of foreign agents or be closed down. Adoption of Russian children by Americans, a widespread practice since the 1990s, was halted. Liberal opposition ceased to exist in Russia as a political fact. Some of its members accepted the Kremlin's offer to serve in the government and joined the system, others remained active mostly in the social media, and a few left the country.

Yet, politics apart, the arts scene in Russia flourished. The deep crisis of Russian culture in the first half of the 1990s was long forgotten. The rise of Russian capitalism and the emergence of new middle classes supported cinema, theater, literature, and ballet, as well as the popular arts. Creative directors, playwrights, writers, actors, and singers became national icons, and the more successful among them also became very rich. As different ideological currents and value systems began to clash again, the Russian cultural scene became a field for controversy, with conservatives attacking ultra-liberals, who in their turn were actively pushing the boundaries of the acceptable.

Breaking Out of the Post-Cold War Order

In 2014, Russia's foreign policy took a sharp turn that led to its confrontation with the United States and alienation from much of Europe. In response to the upheaval in Kiev, which toppled the regime of Viktor Yanukovych and installed a coalition of pro-Western forces and anti-Russian nationalists, President Putin sent forces to Crimea, who secured the peninsula for a referendum in favor of joining Russia, and then materially supported anti-Kiev rebels in Donbass in Ukraine's east who refused to submit to the new Ukrainian regime and formed separatist entities. Thus, Russia broke out of the post-Cold War system in Europe and openly and forcefully challenged the US-dominated world order.

This breakout did not come from nowhere. Russia's relations with the West had been strained for years prior to the Ukraine crisis. The root cause of the conflict between Moscow and Washington was the inability of the two Cold War antagonists to agree on an acceptable security relationship between them once their four-decades-long confrontation was over. The United States, convinced that it had won the Cold War, expected Russia to accept its new role as Washington's subordinate in world affairs. Russia, thinking that the Cold War had been ended by joint agreement, aspired to the position of joint leader with the United States of the new order. When Moscow realized this was not possible, it resolved not to submit its own national interests to those of Washington. To yield to that, however, was for Washington akin to abdication of its global hegemony. Hence the clash.

In reality, this was not so straightforward. When Putin first came to office, he tried hard to integrate Russia with the United States and Europe. After the terrorist attacks of September 11, 2001, he immediately reached out to President George W. Bush and gave the United States real and valuable support for the operation in Afghanistan. In October 2001, Putin delivered a speech to the German Bundestag, in German, in which he proclaimed Russia's "European choice." Already from 2000, Putin had been probing the NATO secretary general and the alliance's leaders about the possibility of Russian membership. He was even willing to tolerate the US withdrawal from the

Anti-Ballistic Missile Treaty that had been in force since 1972; US troop deployments in Central Asia and Georgia; and the inclusion in 2004 of the Baltic States in NATO.

The results of these conciliatory moves, however, fell short of the Kremlin's expectations. Already from 2002, the Bush administration became focused on Iraq and lost interest in a strategic partnership with Russia. The European Union offered Russia "common spaces" but no institutional link. NATO agreed to a new supposedly inclusive format of relations with Russia, but it did not provide for the joint decision-making that Moscow coveted. The reason given for these limits on partnership was Russia's slow progress toward a democratic polity based on the rule of law, and even backsliding to authoritarianism (after the 2003 Yukos case). The deeper rationale was perhaps fear, not unfounded, that Russia's full membership in Western institutions would dilute US leadership and even lead to a fragmentation of the West: the Franco-German–Russian joint opposition to the 2003 US–UK invasion of Iraq had acted as a bit of a wake-up call.

Even though the Bush administration did not punish the Kremlin too severely for its position on Iraq, US–Russian relations took a turn for the worse. Moscow saw Washington's hands at work in the color revolutions, and interpreted the Orange upheaval in Kiev as, at a minimum, an attempt to ease Russia out of Ukraine, or, worse, a dress rehearsal of a "regime change" in Russia itself. In his speech after the terrorist attack in Beslan, Putin blamed the United States, without naming it, for attempts to weaken Russia. As Western criticism of the Kremlin's increasing authoritarianism grew, Moscow imposed restrictions on foreign-funded NGOs. Relations with the EU, which reached their peak with the agreement on common spaces, stagnated as European delegates began to raise the "values gap" in their meetings with their Russian counterparts, still officially called strategic partners.

For the Western media, Putin's 2006 public comment on the passing of the Soviet Union as a major catastrophe of the twentieth century served as a certificate of his imperial, if not Communist, nostalgia. Russia's public image in the West began to sink to the level of the Soviet Union's. The assassinations in 2006 in Moscow of a noted investigative journalist and Kremlin critic, Anna Politkovskaya, and then, in London, of a former KGB officer, Alexander Litvinenko, were blamed on the Russian security services, the Kremlin, and even on Putin personally. For his part, Putin, speaking in February 2007 at the Munich Security Conference, lashed out at the United States' hegemonic practices in world affairs.

The Georgia War and the Ukraine Crisis

The biggest issue at the time in Russian–Western relations was the desire for NATO membership by Ukraine and Georgia – both of which had had successful color revolutions. In the spring of 2008, Putin even came to the NATO summit in Bucharest – the first and only time he did this – to warn Western leaders about the dangers of Ukraine's disintegration in the event of a new round of enlargement. His admonitions, however, were interpreted as bullying, actually strengthening the case for Ukraine's integration into the Western alliance. While Germany and France blocked awarding Kiev and Tbilisi a US-backed Membership Action Plan (MAP) to join the alliance, a compromise was reached which was perhaps the worst of both worlds: no MAP for either country, but a promise to eventually admit them to NATO.

Already in August 2008, tensions between Georgia and Russia had led to a military conflict. Georgian President Mikheil Saakashvili, encouraged by what he interpreted as strong US support, used force in an attempt to restore Tbilisi's control over a tiny breakaway region of South Ossetia, protected by Russian peacekeepers. The plan was to overwhelm the region before the arrival of Russian troops from across the Caucasus, and to put pressure on Moscow to cede control over the other separatist enclave of Abkhazia, thus eliminating the two obstacles in the way of Georgia's NATO accession. At the time, Putin was participating in the opening of the Olympics in Beijing, while Medvedev was vacationing on the Volga.

Saakashvili's plan did not work. Russian forces swiftly crossed the border from the north and defeated the Georgians in the five-day war, coming within less than an hour's drive from Tbilisi. The United States condemned the Russian action and demonstrated its support for Georgia, but did not intervene. France, acting on behalf of the EU, helped Russia and Georgia negotiate a cease-fire. Moscow then recognized South Ossetia and Abkhazia as sovereign states, thus redrawing the post-Soviet borders for the first time, and deployed military bases in the two areas.

What followed after the shock of Russia's first war against a former Soviet neighbor was not Moscow's isolation but a sudden improvement in its relations with the United States and the EU. In early 2009, Barack Obama, who replaced George W. Bush as US president, proclaimed a "reset" of Washington's policy toward Russia. For their part, the Europeans, led by Germany, announced "modernization partnerships" with Russia. Both Americans and Europeans placed hopes on Russia's new nominal leader, President Medvedev, whom they regarded as more liberal and more modern than Putin. This opened the last episode in post-Soviet Russia's quest to form a stable partnership with the West. The episode, however, did not last long.

In 2010, Russia and the United States signed an agreement to reduce strategic nuclear arms – a New START treaty. Later in the same year, Russia and NATO adopted a declaration on strategic partnership. They even engaged in discussions about a joint ballistic missile defense architecture in Europe, which would place the former Cold War opponents within a common defense perimeter. In early 2011, Moscow, for the first and only time, decided not to stay in the way of a Western military intervention in a third country, by abstaining during a UN Security Council vote on a no-fly zone in Libya. This, however, was as far as things could progress.

On the Road to Confrontation with the United States

In 2012, as Putin returned to the Kremlin and the United States entered a presidential election campaign, the mood changed. Relations between Moscow and Washington were put on hold, while critics became more active. Concerned about the Arab Spring and reeling from the way things in Libya had turned out, Russia hardened its stance on Syria, a former Soviet client. Putin gave Syrian President Bashar al-Assad political backing and military aid to stand up to the armed opposition supported by the West. Dismay in the United States and Europe over Putin's return was palpable. By the end of the year, the long-awaited repeal of the almost 40-year-old Jackson–Vanik amendment restricting US trade with Moscow became a farce as it was replaced with the new Magnitsky Act imposing fresh US sanctions on those accused of human rights violations in Russia.

The following year, deterioration of relations became critical as US and Russian policies in Syria began to diverge even more. Moscow even managed to stay Washington's hand, which was already prepared to punish Damascus for its alleged use of chemical weapons. Russia proposed a plan to rid Syria of its chemical arsenal, which was accepted by the United States and implemented. American public opinion, however, judged this to be a ruse by Moscow which exposed President Obama as a weak leader. Just before this, Russia refused to extradite Edward Snowden, a CIA contractor determined to reveal US intelligence secrets to the world. This was interpreted as a clear slap in the face of the US administration.

In Europe, Moscow and Brussels engaged in a geo-political competition over the EU's offer of an association agreement with Ukraine. Moscow, which was trying to include Ukraine into its own economic bloc, the Eurasian Economic Union, sought to become a third party to the Kiev–Brussels talks, which the Europeans rejected. Russia then pressured Kiev to suspend its economic association bid with the EU. This in turn provoked mass demonstrations in the Ukrainian capital, which the police tried to put down with the use of force. Police violence led to more protests, which resulted in a permanent demonstration in Kiev's main square, the Maidan Nezalezhnosti, during the winter of 2013–14.

With the relations with the West becoming more strained, Russia, after several false starts, began reforming its military in earnest. The Georgia war of 2008, which exposed some serious drawbacks in the Russian military organization, stimulated the move. Within five years, the Russian armed forces managed to transform themselves from a decaying post-Soviet structure into a usable instrument of Moscow's foreign and security policy. Weaponry and equipment were modernized; the troops and forces resumed regular exercises; and the pay and living conditions of the officer corps were substantially improved to make service more attractive. In 2010, a major 10-year program of military modernization was announced which is running to this day.

Even as the Maidan protests were raging, Putin was hosting the Winter Olympics in Sochi, on Russia's Black Sea coast. These were only the second Games staged in Russia, after the ill-starred 1980 Moscow Summer Olympics. The Kremlin hoped to roll out the image of a "modern Russia," and spent lavishly on the preparations. However, with relations with the West strained, most European and North American leaders chose to shun the ceremonies. On the closing day of the Games, the Ukrainian leadership of President Viktor Yanukovych, who had been trying to balance between Russia and the West, was toppled by the Maidan protests. Putin watched the worst possible scenario becoming a reality: power in the biggest post-Soviet neighbor country being seized by a coalition of pro-Western elites and virulently anti-Russian Ukrainian nationalists.

Putin reacted immediately by sending more forces to Crimea, where Russia had had a naval base in Sevastopol, to secure the peninsula. Shortly after, a referendum in the majority-Russian region yielded a vote in favor of joining the Russian Federation. Moreover, refusing to recognize the new authorities in Kiev, Moscow supported anti-Maidan elements in eastern Ukraine, encouraging them to organize a new entity in the south-east of the country, Novorossiya (New Russia). This involved Russia – both directly and indirectly – in an armed conflict in Ukraine's eastern border region, Donbass. While the level of violence was reduced by the 2015 Minsk agreement, by now the conflict has claimed well over 10,000 lives and produced over a million displaced persons and refugees, many of whom fled to Russia.

Hybrid War

After 2014, Russia's relations with the United States remained confrontational, while relations with EU countries became marked by mutual alienation and estrangement. This had important implications for Russia's foreign policy as a whole. Moscow's post-Soviet quest for integration with Europe and a security partnership with the United States was finally abandoned. Russia and the West found themselves in a situation reminiscent of the Cold War, though differing from it in many important ways – a "hybrid war," as I call it. Simultaneously, the Ukraine crisis delivered the *coup de grâce* to Russia's effort to reintegrate the former Soviet republics. Having shed illusions about becoming part of the West and finally buried its imperialist ambitions, Russia was on its own.

Yet Moscow was by no means completely isolated. Its relations with China had grown closer, even if this new rapprochement could not compensate for the rupture with the West. Moscow and Beijing have long officially regarded each other as strategic partners, but their actual relationship is more intimate, something that may be called entente. Should there be more pressure on both China and Russia coming from the United States, which now sees both countries as rivals and adversaries, alliance-type elements may emerge in the Sino-Russian relationship, where Beijing, rather than Moscow, is the more dynamic and powerful partner. Russia's traditionally close relations with India are another major foreign policy resource.

Russia's foreign policy activism made itself felt in the Middle East, where Moscow intervened in 2015 in the war in Syria, in which it helped defeat the rebels and Islamist extremists fighting against President Bashar al-Assad. This intervention saved the Assad regime and undercut the post-Cold War de facto Western monopoly on military action in the region – much to the dismay and disappointment of the United States and Europe. The Syria intervention signaled Moscow's comeback as a great power. Since 2017, the US government has officially regarded it as a rival and strategic competitor.[4]

Apart from its actions in Ukraine and Syria, Russia was accused of meddling in the 2016 US presidential elections in favor of Donald Trump, and of collusion with Trump himself. In 2018, the UK authorities accused Russian military intelligence of nerve-gas poisonings in Britain. Several European governments made accusations of Russian interference in their domestic political processes. Moscow flatly denied all charges. Yet the very nature of hybrid war makes the global information space and essentially borderless cyberspace prime battlefields in the new confrontation. Since 2012 at the latest, the Russian state-run media have adopted a more aggressive stance toward the West. From the Kremlin's point of view, the United States, which routinely interferes abroad, can hardly claim inviolability of its own domestic turf.

The Kremlin's interventions in Ukraine and Syria and its interference in the West have led to waves of anti-Russian sanctions. The sanctions have not, however, resulted either in a reversal of Moscow's foreign policy course; a fragmentation of the Russian political regime; or a collapse of the Russian economy. In the short term, they resulted in the rallying of the Russian people around the flag and Putin as a symbol of patriotism. In the 2018 presidential elections, Putin collected over 75% of the vote with almost 70% turnout, thus for the first time getting the support of an absolute majority of registered voters. Foreign restrictions on wealthy Russians have even helped the Kremlin's effort to discipline – "nationalize" – Russian elites. Yet in the longer term the sanctions burden, which will only grow over time, will take a heavy toll on investment resources, technological capability, and economic opportunities available to Russia. Sanctions contribute to tensions with Russia's economy, society, and polity.

Putin's fourth presidential term started with the controversy over the increase in the pension age. The president took the responsibility for the unpopular measure, and was willing to pay with a 20% drop in public support. Even with that, of course, he can effectively rule Russia, relying on a popular approval of 60%. The larger issue behind the pension reform is high inequality and runaway official corruption. Putin's legacy will be judged by whether he manages to reduce the former and tame the latter. It is true that Russians have never had it so good – materially or spiritually – in absolute terms, but it is the relative that often matters to people more.

So long as Vladimir Putin remains in power in Russia this chapter will remain unfinished. Putin is not a man of ideology, vision, or trenchant ideas. He is, above all, a pragmatist. His actions are guided by his understanding of Russia's national interest. Putin has accomplished a great deal for Russia, having appeared on the scene as the right man at a critically important juncture, as the country was facing the prospect of disintegration for the second time in a decade. He has his failings and limitations. Out of chaos he built a regime. Transforming this regime into a state will be a task for his successors. Only time will tell if this is a feasible undertaking.

Conclusion: Forever Russia

Russia's twentieth-century history is full of drama. The people of Russia brought down the state twice on their own heads, each time hoping for a brighter future. In both cases, the change was unthinkable right before it became inevitable. In the writer Ivan Bunin's memorable words, in February 1917 "Russia sneaked away in three days." In August 1991, it also took three days for the ill-fated "putsch" designed to save the Soviet Union to destroy it. Both in 1917 and in 1991, the Russian state collapsed because the people of Russia had lost confidence in their rulers, and withdrew respect from the system which those rulers embodied.

Each time a version of the Time of Troubles followed. Periods of anarchy were devastating, but in the end the state managed to reassert itself. The first time Russia re-emerged as a totalitarian Communist state that boasted tremendous achievements domestically and internationally, for which, however, the Russian people had to pay a horrendous price. The second time it led to an authoritarian regime promoting consumerism and allowing a high degree of personal freedom, but also demonstrating a high degree of inequality and injustice.

Historically, Russia has been governed in an authoritarian fashion – whatever the political system or the ideology of its rulers: Orthodox monarchy, Soviet Communism, or crony capitalism. This mode of governance abhors alternatives – until the change of the ruler, or of the entire political system, or of the political regime, which, for the duration of its dominance, equally abhors alternatives. This modus operandi of the rulers is upheld by deep-seated fears among the people of domestic turmoil or foreign invasion. These fears are gradually subsiding, but the fundamental principle of unity of state power is unlikely to change in the next several decades. There is a major issue, however, with the way power is exercised.

Present-day Russia has reinstated authority, but not really the state as such. In its place, the elites have installed a governing system that absolves them of responsibility while serving their interests. This triumph of the elites over the state is historically un-Russian as the elites, for all their privileges, have always been servants of the state, and it is hardly sustainable in the long term. The state will likely be back, but what kind of a state? Ideally, it should be a driver of development and progress, and a partner for business and civil society. Such a state could play the leading role in transforming and upgrading the Russian economy, technology, and society itself. For this, the future Russian state needs to be a meritocratic system built on equality before the law, an independent judiciary, self-governance, and national solidarity. Of course, there are other, less appealing alternatives.

The ups and downs in Russian history have been closely connected with dominant figures. The issue of leadership has been crucial. One person's actions or inaction may decide whether the country continues to exist. Strong leaders have compensated for weak and incapable elites, although often at a high cost for the people, but weak leaders have usually spelled utter calamity if they happened to rule at the time of crisis. The Russian Empire was not doomed to go under in 1917; nor was the Soviet Union – at least before 1989. It was the loss of control by Nicholas II and Mikhail Gorbachev – both admirable people in other respects – that sealed the country's fate. The system will take its next fateful test when Vladimir Putin leaves the political stage. It will be the result of this test that will seal his legacy.

The salient feature of Russian history, which also made itself felt twice in the twentieth century, has been the country's ability to rise again after a devastating catastrophe. Russia briefly ceased to exist, as a coherent whole, after the 1917 revolution; it almost ceased to exist in the late 1990s. Yet each time it managed to coalesce and even claim a major international role. Russia acted in the twentieth century as a country with a truly global reach. Inspired by Communist ideology, it set itself the impossible goal to be a model and a trailblazer for humanity, and although it did not reach that goal, its impact and achievements were truly astounding. Even though Russia is much smaller today relative to other world powers, it has retained a strong sense of independence, a global outlook, and a particular brand of exceptionalism based on its prevailing faith, remarkable geography, and rich experience.

In Russia, politics usually trumps economics. Not that economic conditions are unimportant – food riots sparked the revolution in February 1917, and food shortages in 1990–1 contributed to the downfall of the Communist regime – but improving material well-being is not the end goal of Russian society. This is also one reason why the Western sanctions imposed on Russia after 2014 have not worked as expected. Traditional Russian culture does not glorify private wealth-creation, and extolls self-sacrifice for a good cause. This is changing, but self-enrichment is unlikely to be the end goal of most Russians. What keeps Russian people together is a particular form of spiritual bonds whose main ingredients are a long historical tradition centered on the state; a sense of cultural distinction, even uniqueness; and a certain standing and mission in the world as an independent global actor.

After Putin

The Putin era continues, even though its end is already in sight. Vladimir Putin is unlikely to become president for life. Indeed, he has become the first Russian leader who is actually busy grooming a whole next generation of Russian leaders. Lenin, from his death-bed, tried to influence the configuration of a future Communist Party leadership – in vain. Stalin, also in the final months of his life, sought to bring new blood to the party's ruling organ, and then cleanse it of the blood of the old guard, but he too died before he could complete his plan. Putin began his work in the mid-2010s, when he was just over 60, well ahead of his 2018 re-election to a new six-year term.

It may be that he hands the presidency to a chosen successor, flanked by other next-generation people, in 2024, while continuing to exercise general oversight, as a kind of president mentor, Singaporean-style, or as a supreme leader, or even – though far less likely – as a party chief à la Sonia Gandhi's India or contemporary Poland. Today, the talk of the town is that Putin heads the revamped Council of State that would have the position of a supreme guide and arbiter enshrined in a revised constitution. Perhaps, though this can change. It may be that Putin's effective rule ends in 2030, or earlier, or later. No matter: these things are impossible to predict. What is obvious is that a political transition is inevitable, and with it, the end of a long era, and of a particular kind of political regime.

For the time being, Russia will evolve within the limits imposed by the domestic regime and external circumstances. Internal restrictions rooted in the monopolistic nature of the Russian political-economic regime are far more important. They stifle much of the people's energies, lead to gross underperformance and crass inequality, distort or destroy competition, and make official corruption not a bug in the system but the system itself.

External restrictions resulting from the ongoing confrontation with the United States and alienation from much of Europe push the Kremlin not so much to cleanse the system as to bolster it in the face of its formidable adversary. Even as economic opportunities for Russia are considerably narrowed on the global scene, transformation of the system toward more meritocracy and accountability, better governance, and greater social solidarity is being postponed.

Yet a combination of sluggish economic growth, growing disgruntlement over inequality, injustice, and pervasive official corruption, combined with paternalistic inertia and the elites' aloofness and unwillingness to change, plus the ever-heavier burden of sanctions, might produce an upheaval just at the point when the political situation finally creates an opening for reform.

A political crisis following Putin's final departure is virtually pre-programmed. Power in Russia is tightly intertwined with property ownership, so that any political change would usher in a redistribution of wealth. The political economy of Russia is a constantly changing kaleidoscope, with tactical alliances falling apart as quickly as they emerge. Once the center of the system is replaced, rivalry for the top position may be intense. This rivalry, however, has little to do with the interests of the country and its people.

What is impossible to foresee, however, is its outcome and the future direction of Russian policies. It is a safe bet to say that Russia is unlikely to elect a version of liberal capitalism and agree to some form of political capitulation to the West. Beyond that, there are a range of possibilities. It may well be that the desire to reduce inequality and injustice, curb corruption, and introduce a cleaner and more efficient administration will become the new guiding principle.

It is thus possible that post-Putin Russia will eliminate the remaining vestiges of 1990s-vintage oligarchy and 2000s-vintage cronyism and set about making its state capitalism more efficient, more national, and more humane. The central challenge for post-Putin leaders will be to build a functioning state in Russia, in place of the current political regime posing as a state. Of course, the advent in the 2000s of a political regime in place of the 1990s chaos was a great improvement, but turning the regime into a state – in the sense of disciplining the elites – would be the logical next step, perhaps for the 2030s.

Toward a Russian Federation 2.0

The policies of Russia's future leaders are more likely to lean to the left domestically and toward closer relations with non-Western countries, including China, internationally. Putin's never-to-be-satisfied desire to be "understood" by the United States might be seen by his eventual successors as being akin to appeasement.

In extremis, Alexander Nevsky's hard choice of submitting to the East to fight off the West could be made again. For Russia, it has always been more important to save its soul than its body. The optimal geopolitical construct, however, would be something like a Grand Eurasian equilibrium with Berlin, Beijing, and Delhi becoming Moscow's principal foreign partners.

In the near and possibly medium term, the most important foreign policy task will be avoiding a Russian–American military conflict. In the early twenty-first century, the Moscow–Washington relationship is no longer the most important element of global politics, but it could turn out to be the most dangerous one. If that war can be avoided, and some form of an understanding reached, based on a revised view in the United States of its global role (essentially: from a global hegemon to a primus inter pares), and on Russia's settling into its own new role of a great power of a new type (essentially: national independence rather than regional dominance), the world system will be more stable, and Russia will get a chance to focus on its domestic development.

Indeed, after everything that the country went through in the twentieth century, Russia needs many decades to rehabilitate itself, develop organically, build trust and stimulate cooperation among its own people, make sure that laws apply equally to all, and agree on the basic principles that make up the nation. If the Russian people succeed at that, a new iteration of the Russian Federation – RF 2.0 – may follow. This would actually be in accordance with the country's long historical tradition. Whatever its shape, form, and substance, it will be recognizably Russian. There will always be a Russia. Its own history vouchsafes that.

Further Reading

There is a virtual glut of literature in English on twentieth-century Russia. To begin with, I would recommend Geoffrey Hosking's *Russian History: A Very Short Introduction* (Oxford University Press, 2012) and his two major works: *Russia: People and Empire* (Harvard University Press, 1998), which covers the period from the 1552 conquest of Kazan – which marks the beginning of the Russian Empire – to 1917; and *The First Socialist Society: A History of the Soviet Union from Within*, which follows up through the early 1980s (Fontana Press/Collins, 1985).

In my judgment, the best books in English about the Russian Empire and its demise are both by Dominic Lieven: *The Russian Empire and Its Rivals* (John Murray, 2000) and *The End of Tsarist Russia: The March Toward World War I and the Revolution* (Penguin, 2015). Russia's tortuous path toward the Bolshevik revolution is vividly described by Orlando Figes in *A People's Tragedy: The Russian Revolution 1891–1924* (Penguin, 1996).

Soviet history is perhaps best captured by the biographies of the Communist leaders. On Lenin, I would recommend Dmitri Volkogovov's *Lenin: A New Biography* (Simon and Schuster, 1998) and

Robert Service's *Lenin* (Pan Books, 2008); on Trotsky, Volkogonov's *Trotsky: The Eternal Revolutionary* (The Free Press, 1996) and Service's *Trotsky: A Biography* (Macmillan, 2009); on Bukharin, Stephen F. Kotkin's *Bukharin and the Bolshevik Revolution* (Oxford University Press, 1973); on Stalin, Volkognov's *Stalin: Triumph and Tragedy* (Phoenix, 2000), Service's *Stalin* (Belknap Press, 2006), Simon Sebag Montefiore's *Young Stalin* (Weidenfeld & Nicolson, 2007) and *Stalin: The Court of the Red Tsar* (Weidenfeld & Nicolson, 2003), and Kotkin's *Stalin, Vol. I: Paradoxes of Power, 1878–1928* (Allen Lane, 2014) and *Stalin, Vol. II: Waiting for Hitler, 1929–1941* (Penguin, 2017); on Khrushchev, William Taubman's *Khrushchev: The Man and His Era* (Norton, 2003); on Gorbachev, Taubman's *Gorbachev: His Life and Times* (Norton, 2017); on Yeltsin, Leon Aron's, *Yeltsin: A Revolutionary Life* (HarperCollins, 2000); and on Putin, Angus Roxburgh's *The Strongman: Vladimir Putin and the Struggle for Russia* (Macmillan, 2013). For a wider focus, I would address readers to Volkogonov's *Autopsy for an Empire: The Seven Leaders Who Built the Soviet Regime* (Simon and Schuster, 1995) and Archie Brown's *The Rise and Fall of Communism* (Ecco, 2009).

The more valuable books on specific phenomena of Soviet Russian history include Robert Conquest's *The Great Terror* (Oxford University Press, 1968); Alexander Werth's *Russia at War, 1941–1945* (Barrie and Rockliff, 1964); and Rodric Braithwaite's *Afgantsy: The Russians in Afghanistan, 1979–1989* (Profile Books, 2011). Eyewitness accounts of the end of the

Communist system can be found in the books by the US ambassador to Russia, Jack Matlock, *An Autopsy on an Empire* (Random House, 1995); and his UK colleague, Rodric Braithwaite, *Across the Moscow River: The World Turned Upside Down* (Yale University Press, 2002). Also to be recommended are the books by the American journalist David Remnick, *Lenin's Tomb: The Last Days of the Soviet Empire* (Vintage, 1993), and the head of the US National Security Agency, General William Odom's *The Collapse of the Soviet Military* (Yale University Press, 1998), which describes the disintegration of one of the most powerful military establishments in history. The rise of new Russian capitalism is dissected by David Hoffman in *The Oligarchs: Wealth and Power in the New Russia* (Public Affairs, 2011).

The best books on Russian culture and society include *Natasha's Dance: A Cultural History of Russia* (Metropolitan Books, 2002) by Orlando Figes; and *The Icon and the Axe: An Interpretive History of Russian Culture* (Vintage, 1970) and *Russia in Search of Itself* (Woodrow Wilson Center Press, 2004), both by James Billington.

I could also mention, humbly, my own book, *Post-Imperium: A Eurasian Story* (Carnegie Endowment, 2012), which describes the country's post-imperial travails.

Nothing, of course, can replace reading Russian authors whose literary works make their country's history a truly living thing. My favorites include Mikhail Bulgakov's *The White Guard* and *Heart of a Dog*;

Mikhail Sholokhov's *And Quiet Flows the Don*; Boris Pasternak's *Doctor Zhivago*; Vasily Grosman's *Life and Fate*; and the many works by Alexander Solzhenitsyn, from *One Day in the Life of Ivan Denisovich* to *The Red Wheel* and *The Gulag Archipelago*.

Notes

Introduction: Russia's Many Russias

1 *Bol'shaya Sovetskaya Entsiklopedia*, 2nd edition, vol. 2, Moscow: BSE Publishers, 1950, pp. 22–3.

Chapter 1 Revolutionary Upheaval (1901–20)

1 "Rossiya," *Entsiklopedicheskiy slovar*, St. Petersburg: F.A. Brockhaus/I.A. Efron Publishers, 1898, pp. 75, 76.
2 Ibid., p. 86.
3 A.B. Zubov (ed.), *Istoriya Rossii. XX vek: 1894–1939*, Moscow: Astrel, 2009, pp. 69, 72.
4 Ibid., pp. 82, 88.
5 Deutsche Bank, *The World Economy, a Millennial Perspective*, Paris: OECD, 2001.
6 Lenin, "Lecture on the 1905 Revolution," remarks addressed to young Swiss workers, January 22, 1917, first published in *Pravda* 18, January 22, 1925: *Lenin Collected Works*, vol. 23, Moscow: Progress Publishers, 1964, pp. 236–53. See also E.H. Carr, *The Bolshevik Revolution 1917–1923*, vol. 1, London: Pelican, 1973, p. 80.
7 Lenin, "O zadachakh proletariata v dannoy revolyutsii!" *Pravda*, April 20, 1917.
8 Carr, *The Bolshevik Revolution*, vol. 1, p. 104.
9 Ibid., p. 120.

Chapter 2 The Rise of the Soviet State (1921–38)

1 Zubov (ed.), *Istoriya Rossii, XX vek: 1894–1939*, pp. 819–20.
2 Stephen Kotkin, *Stalin: Vol. 2. Waiting for Hitler, 1929–1941*, New York: Penguin Press, 2017, p. 305.

3 I.V. Stalin, *Voprosy leninizma*, Leningrad: Partizdat, 1935, p. 445.

4 Zubov (ed.), *Istoriya Rossii*, pp. 910–11.

5 A statement by the State Duma of the Russian Federation, April 2, 2008, No. 262-5 GD, "In Memoriam of the Victims of the 1930s Famine in the Territory of the USSR" (in Russian).

6 V.P. Popov, "Gosudarstvenny terror v sovetskoy Rossii 1923–1953," *Otechestvennye arkhivy*, 2, 1992.

7 See, for example, Varlam Shalamov's *Kolymya Stories* (1968) and Evgenia Ginzburg's *Within the Whirlwind* (1973).

8 According to the 1920 partial census and 1937 universal census results.

9 *Istoriya Vsesoyuznoy kommunisticheskoy partii (bolshevikov). Kratkiy kurs*, Moscow: Gospolitizdat, 1938.

10 V.I. Lenin, *Collected Works*, vol. 44, 5th edition, Moscow: Politizdat, 1970, p. 579 (in Russian).

11 Maxim Gorky, "Esli vrag ne sdayotsya, ego unichtozhayut," *Pravda*, November 15, 1930.

12 Zubov (ed.), *Istoriya Rossii, XX vek: 1894–1939*, p. 964.

13 "My rozhdeny, chtob skazku sdelat' byuliyu ..." – a line from the "Aviators' March," a 1920s song of the Soviet Air Force.

Chapter 3 World War II and Its Aftermath (1939–52)

1 See Valentin Berezhkov, *S diplomaticheskoy missiey v Berlin, 1940–1941*, Moscow: APN Publishers, 1967.

2 The figures were released in 2011 by the interagency commission for counting the losses during the 1941–5 war.

3 Except for the United States, which never recognized the Soviet annexation of the Baltic States.

4 Stalin's speech in Moscow on February 9, 1946; Churchill's speech at Fulton, Missouri, on March 5, 1946.

5 Walter Lippman, *The Cold War: A Study in US Foreign Policy*, New York: Harper and Brothers, 1947.

6 Vladislav Zubok and Constantine Pleshakov, *Inside the Kremlin's Cold War: From Stalin to Khrushchev*, Cambridge, Mass.: Harvard University Press, 2003.

7 Vladimir Kuznechevskiy, *Leningradskoe Delo*, Moscow: Russian Institute for Strategic Studies, 2017.

8 The Soviet prosecutor general's memorandum to Nikita Khrushchev, February 1, 1954. See V.N. Zemskov, "Zaklyuchennye v 1930-e gody: sotsialno-ekonomicheskie problem," *Otechestvennaya Istoriya*, 4, 1997, p. 67.

Chapter 4 Mature Socialism and Its Stagnation (1953–84)

1 CPSU General Secretary Yuri V. Andropov's remarks at the Plenary Session of the Central Committee of the Communist Party of the Soviet Union, *Pravda*, November 23, 1982.

Chapter 5 Democratic Upheaval (1985–99)

1 According to the official figures of the Russian Ministry of Defense.
2 Andrei Zubov (ed.), *Istoriya Rossii. XX vek. 1939–2007*, Moscow: Astrel, 2009, pp. 648–51.
3 Ibid., p. 613.

Chapter 6 From Stability to Uncertainty (2000–19)

1 Vladimir Putin (with Nataliya Gevorkyan, Natalya Timakova, and Andrei Kolesnikov), *First Person: An Astonishingly Frank Self-Portrait by Russia's President Vladimir Putin*, translated by Catherine A. Fitzpatrick, New York: Public Affairs, 2000, pp. 139–42.
2 Ekaterina Mereminskaya, "Gosudarstvo i goskompanii kontroliruyut 70% rossiyskoy ekonomiki," *Vedomosti*, September 29, 2016.
3 Zubov (ed.), *Istoriya Rossii. XX vek. 1939–2007*, p. 648,
4 See the US National Security Strategy (December 2017), the US National Defense Strategy (January 2018), and the Nuclear Posture Review (February 2018).

Index

A-bomb 92
Abkhazia 128, 141, 146, 168, 169
Abramovich, Roman 137, 156
absolute monarchy 17–18, 19, 48
Abuladze, Tenghiz 124
Adenauer, Konrad 108
adoption of children 163
Afanasiev, Yuri 127
Afghanistan
  Comintern 73
  intervention in 113, 116, 142
  jihadism 117
  USA 165
  withdrawal from 130, 132
Africa 109, 116, 132
agriculture
  collectivization 63–5, 103–4
  Khrushchev 103–4
  Land Question 21
  national project 161
  production 61, 118
  rebuilding of 90
  Stolypin 28
  war communism 52
  World War I 33
  see also peasantry
Akhmadulina, Bella 105

Akhmatova, Anna 69, 94
Aksyonov, Vasily 105
Alaska 16
Albania 91, 109
Alekperov, Vagit 137
Alexander II, Tsar 20
Alexander III, Tsar 19
Alexandra Feodorovna, Empress 32
Alexandrov, Grigory 69
Alexeyev, Mikhail 44
Alexy II, Patriarch 147, 162–3
Algeria 109–10
All Union Communist Party 71
And Quiet Flows the Don (Sholokov) 69
Andropov, Yuri 118–19, 122
Anglo-French coalition 77, 81
Anti-Ballistic Missile Treaty 165–6
Anti-Comintern Pact 74
anti-fascism 73, 96
anti-Hitler coalition 85
anti-Soviet agitation trials 114
Arab Spring 170
Armenia 16, 31, 42, 54, 128, 130
arms exports 158
arts 24, 69, 106, 147, 164

Asia 9–10, 54, 73, 92, 109
  see also Eurasia
al-Assad, Bashar 170, 174
assassination 26, 167
atheism, official 12, 43, 51,
    70, 147
Atlantic Charter 85
Attlee, Clement 88
Austria 25, 30, 108
autarky 62, 118
authoritarianism 13, 48–9,
    166, 167, 177–8
autocracy 11, 19, 48
Azerbaijan 16, 42, 54, 141

Balkans 24, 25, 29, 146
  see also individual countries
Ballets russes 24
ballistic missile defense
    169–70
Baltic States
  Brest-Litovsk treaty 41
  Germans driven out 86
  Gorbachev 130
  independence 45, 128
  mutual assistance treaties
    79–80
  Stalin 78
  Wehrmacht 84
  see also individual countries
banishment 58, 95, 96, 97
  see also exile
banks 157–8
Barbarossa plan 82–3, 84
Basayev, Shamil 149
Battleship Potemkin (Eisenstein)
    27, 68
BBC Russian Service 124–5

Belarus 3, 4, 16, 54
  Brest-Litovsk treaty 41, 134
  energy exports 146
  ethnicity 17, 79
  Germany 30, 86
  nuclear powerplant
    explosion 123
  nuclear weapons 146
  Wehrmacht 84
Berdyaev, Nikolai 23, 75
Berezovsky, Boris 137, 150
Beria, Lavrentiy 1–2, 92, 96,
    100
Berlin 88, 92, 109
Berlin Wall 109, 131
Beslan terrorist attack 167
Bessarabia 42, 45, 79, 80
Blavatsky, Helena 23
Blitzkrieg 82, 84
Blok, Alexander 23–4
Bloody Sunday 26
Bolotnaya Square protests
    161, 163
Bolsheviks
  army 37–8, 39
  Communist Party 74–5
  Constituent Assembly 40–1
  culture 65–9
  financial resources 39
  foreign forces 45
  Germany 41, 72
  history 67
  Lenin 33, 36, 38–40, 47
  post-Civil War 51
  Red Terror 43
  religious faith 70
  Russian Orthodox Church
    43

socialism 51–2
Western intervention 45–6
Whites 43–4
Bolshevism 8, 12, 21, 27, 30, 33
Bolshoi ballet 106
Bondarchuk, Sergei 115
Bosporus 25
bourgeoisie 21–2, 55
Brandt, Willi 116
Brest 83
Brest-Litovsk treaty 41–2, 72
Brezhnev, Leonid 96, 112–13, 114–15, 118
Britain 25, 72, 73, 175
Brodsky, Joseph 94, 105
Bryusov, Valery 23–4
Bukhara 18
Bukharin, Nikolai 59
Bukovina, northern 80
Bulgakov, Mikhail 45, 69–70
Bulgakov, Serge 23
Bulgaria 86, 88, 91, 109
Bunin, Ivan 23, 75, 177
Bush, George H. W. 131–2
Bush, George W. 165, 166
Byzantine Empire 6

Cambodia 132
capitalism 14–15, 178, 183
    see also state capitalism
Carter, Jimmy 116
censorship 115, 124
Center for Strategic Research 157
Central America 132

Central Committee 53, 112, 113
Chagall, Marc 24, 75
Chaliapin, Feodor 75
Chechnya
    ethnicity 97
    exile 104
    Georgia 141
    independence 141–2
    Islamism 142–3
    Putin 149, 153–4, 155
    separatists 142–3, 148, 149
Chekah (OGPU) 54
Chekhov, Anton 20, 23
Chemezov, Sergei 155
Chernenko, Konstantin 119–20, 122
Chernobyl explosion 123
Chernomyrdin, Viktor 139, 144
The Cherry Orchard (Chekhov) 20
Chiang Kai-shek 73–4
Chicherin, Georgi 72
children's organizations 66
China
    Harbin 16
    industrialization 93
    Liaodong Peninsula 25
    Putin 174
    Russian Federation 174, 183
    USSR 73–4, 91, 111, 117, 132
Chinese Communist Party 92
Chubais, Anatoly 137, 141, 156
churches demolished 68, 70

Churchill, Winston 85, 87, 92
cinema 68–9, 105, 115
CIS (Commonwealth of Independent States) 134, 146
Civil War 12, 42–5, 54–5, 101
Cold War 13, 92, 93, 116, 132, 165
collective leadership 112
collectivization 12, 63–5, 103–4
Comintern 71, 73, 85
Commonwealth of Independent States (CIS) 134, 146
Communism 103, 104, 179–80
Communist federalism 55
Communist Manifesto (Marx & Engels) 40
Communist Party
  banned and revived 138
  Bolsheviks 74–5
  Central Committee 53
  Civil War 54–5
  collapse of 11, 14
  constitution 60
  democratic platform 127
  elections 140, 152
  ideology 76
  illiteracy 65
  indoctrination 65
  KGB 102
  Khrushchev 101
  and Kremlin 162
  propaganda 1–2
  Red Army 44–5
  Russian Empire 54–5
  Soviet system 53
  on Stalin 101
  "storming the sky" 52
  totalitarianism 177
  world revolution 71
Congress of People's Deputies 126–7, 138
Congress of Soviets 40–1
Constantinople 6–7, 31, 45
Constituent Assembly 35, 37, 39, 40–1
constitution
  abolition of Article 6 127
  elections 159
  first Soviet 41
  Gorbachev 130
  Nicholas II 27
  persecutions 114
  Putin 151, 160–1, 181
  secession rights 57
  Stalin 60
  Yeltsin 138–40, 142
Constitutional Democrats 27
consumerism 103, 158
corruption 98, 120–1, 158, 176, 182–3
cosmism 23
Council of People's Commissars 38
Council of State 152, 181
counter-revolutionary crimes 54, 97
CPSU: *see* Communist Party
Crimea 45, 91, 112, 164, 172–3

cronyism 178, 183
Cuban missile crisis 110, 116, 119
cultural revolution 65–71
culture
  Bolsheviks 65–9
  Brezhnev 115
  ethnic 56–7
  exchanges 106
  intelligentsia 115
  rise of 20, 22–4, 164
  spiritual bonds 180
  thaw 105
Curzon line 79
Cyrillic alphabet 70
Czechoslovak corps 42–5
Czechoslovakia 73, 88, 91, 109, 113, 117

Dagestan 149
Dardanelles 25, 31
The Days of the Turbins (Bulgakov) 45
de Gaulle, Charles 10, 116
deaths
  counter-revolutionary crimes 97
  from famine 64
  hostages 154
  1904 war 25
  Novocherkassk protests 105
  servicemen in Afghanistan 132
  Soviet-era economy 138
  Time of Troubles 50
  Ukraine conflicts 173
  World War I 30
  World War II 89
  Yeltsin standoff 139
de-colonization 109
defense production 62
Democratic Choice 140
Democratic Russia 127
The Demons (Dostoevsky) 11, 22
Deng Xiaoping 132, 134
Denikin, Anton 44
Diaghilev, Sergei 24
dissidents 69, 92, 113–14
Doctor Zhivago (Pasternak) 106
"Doctors' Plot" 96
Donetsk (Stalino) 102
Dostoevsky, Fyodor 11, 22, 23, 105
double-headed eagle 6, 162
doublethink 115
Dovzhenko, Alexander 68
Dubrovka Theater 154
Dudayev, Dzhokhar 141
Duma 27, 32, 35–8, 140, 152
Dunaevsky, Isaak 69
Dunkirk 81

Eastern Europe
  divided 79
  history politics 2
  NATO 146
  Roman Catholicism 4
  Russian Empire 5, 7
  Soviet soldiers 94
  Soviet sphere of influence 73, 78, 79, 87, 91, 131
  subsidized 109

economic progress
  Brezhnev 114–15
  in crisis 117–18, 125–6
  GDP 28
  Khrushchev 103–5
  oil 158
  politics 180, 181–2
  subsidies 56
  war materiel 89–90
economic reforms 135–6,
    156–8
education 65, 67
Egypt 109–10
Eisenstein, Sergei 27, 68, 71
electoral reform 126–7
elites
  corruption 98, 158
  Gorbachev 120
  great power mentality 145
  Khrushchev 104
  Medvedev 161
  nationalized 175
  present day 178
  Putin 15, 155–6, 172
  regional 155
  religious faith 19
  and Russian people 160
  Stalin 59, 98
  Supreme Soviet 128–9
  see also nomenklatura;
    oligarchs
emigration 12, 47, 66, 75, 91,
    115, 125
émigrés 47–8, 75, 90–1
Engels, Friedrich 40
equality 177, 178
estates 19–22
Estonia 16, 42, 79, 80, 133

ethnic conflicts 128
ethnic diversity 17, 56, 79,
    97, 104
ethnic Russians 17, 95, 129,
    135
Eurasia 10, 13, 16, 91, 171,
    184
Euromissile crisis 119
Europe 9, 10, 116
  see also Eastern Europe
European Union 166, 167,
    171
exceptionalism 6–7, 10, 180
exile 66, 97, 104, 114, 151
  see also banishment

famine 53, 64, 90
Federation Council 140
financial crisis 144, 160–1
Finland
  continuation war 86–7
  independence 42, 45
  Lenin 36–7
  Red Army attack 80
  in Russian Empire 16, 18
  Soviet sphere of influence
    79
  Winter War 80
food program 118
food riots 105, 126, 180
  see also famine
Foreign Intelligence Service
    146
foreign policy
  Gorbachev 130–1, 132
  Khrushchev 108–11
  Middle East 174
  Russian Empire 24–6

Ukraine 164
USSR 71–4
Western integration 145–6
France 29, 30, 73, 81
freedom of conscience law
125

Gagarin, Yuri 103
Gaidai, Leonid 115
Gaidar, Yegor 135–6, 139
Galicia 31
Gazprom 157
GDP (gross domestic product)
28, 138, 157
Geneva conference 108
Genghis Khan 4, 91
Georgia
Chechnya 141
ethnic conflicts 128
Gorbachev 130
independence 42
revolution 159
Russia 168–9
in Russian Empire 16
in Russian Federation 54
Stalin 55, 102
US support 168–9
war 171
German Question 108
Germany
Anglo-French coalition 81
Anti-Comintern Pact 74
Belarus 30, 86
and Bolsheviks 41, 72
Brest-Litovsk treaty 41–2
divided 91
India 82
Lithuania 30

NATO 108
Poland 30, 42, 79, 81
Red Army 78, 88
reunification 132
Russia 29–30, 72, 73
Russian intelligentsia 66
Stalin 77–9
USSR 76, 77, 78–80, 82–4,
108
Wehrmacht 83, 84, 86
Weimar Republic 72–3
see also Nazi Germany
Ginzburg, Evgenia 65
glasnost 14, 98, 123–6
Glinka, Mikhail 71
Gogol, Nikolai 23
Golden Horde 2, 6
Gorbachev, Mikhail
Baltic States 130
electoral reforms 126–7
elites 120
foreign policy 130–1, 132
Georgia 130
intelligentsia 124, 129–30
as leader 8, 95, 120–2,
123–4, 134–5, 179
nomenklatura 129–30
reception in West 130–1
resignation 134–5
Russian Orthodox Church
125
and Yeltsin 95, 126,
129–30, 133, 135, 156
see also glasnost; perestroika
Gorky (Nizhny Novgorod) 68
Gorky, Maxim 23, 69
Gosplan (State Planning
Committee) 62

Govorukhin, Stanislav 124
grain imports 104
Grand Soviet Encyclopaedia
1–2
Great Depression 62
Great Patriotic War 12–13,
84–6, 88–9, 94, 98
Great Terror 59–60, 101
Greece 88
Gref, Herman 155–6
Gromyko, Andrei 108, 111,
130–1
Guinea 109–10
GULAG 12, 54, 64, 97, 101,
102, 105
The Gulag Archipelago
(Solzhenitsyn) 65, 124
Gusinsky, Vladimir 137,
151

Harbin 16
Helsinki Final Act 116
history politics 2
Hitler, Adolf 73, 78, 81–2
hostage-taking 142, 154
housing 104
human rights 114, 116, 170
Hungary 4, 25, 88, 91, 109
Hussein, Saddam 132
hybrid war 173–6
hydrogen bombs 92

illiteracy 65
imports 62–3, 104
In the First Circle
(Solzhenitsyn) 64–5
India 73, 82, 109–10, 174
Indonesia 109–10

industrialization 21, 61–3,
65, 75–6, 93, 103
inequality 15, 136, 159, 176,
177, 182, 183
inflation 136, 144, 157
injustice 74, 177, 182, 183
intelligentsia
culture 115
and dissidents 113–14
ethnic 56
exiled 66
Gorbachev 124, 129–30
Jewish 95
replaced 76
representing common
people 22
International Monetary Fund
137–8, 148
Internationale 56–7, 85
internationalism 47, 51, 55,
70
investment 118, 137, 157,
175
Iran 73
Iraq 166
Islamism 142–3, 149
see also Muslim world
Israel, 91
Ivan III, Grand Duke 5–6
Ivan IV, Duke 6
Ivan Susanin (Glinka) 71

Jackson–Vanik amendment
170
Japan 12, 25–6, 73–4, 92,
108
Jewish Anti-Fascist Committee
96

Jewish people 17, 95, 96
jihadism 117
judiciary 18, 140, 178

Kadyrov, Akhmat 153–4
Kadyrov, Ramzan 154
Kaledin, Alexei 44
Kalinin (Tver) 68
Kaliningrad 91
Kalmyks 104
Kamenev, Lev 58, 59
Kandinsky, Wassily 24, 75
Das Kapital (Marx) 40
Karelia, eastern 80
Kasyanov, Mikhail 153
Kazakhstan 16, 64, 146
Kennedy, John F. 110
Kerensky, Alexander 37, 38
KGB 102
Khasbulatov, Ruslan 139
Khiva khans 18
Khodorkovsky, Mikhail
    151
Khrushchev, Nikita
  agriculture 103–4
  anekdoty 107
  anti-Soviet fears 106
  Communist Party 101
  coup against 111–13
  defense 107–8
  economic/social revival
    103–5
  elites 104
  foreign policy 108–11
  gaining power 100
  gold reserves 118
  and Mao 111
  religion 106–7

  Stalin's repression 97,
    101–2
  uprisings 109
  voluntarism 111–12
Khutsiev, Marlen 105
Kiev–Brussels talks 171
Kievan Rus 2, 3, 4, 6–7
Kim Il Sung 92
Kirill, Patriarch 163
Kiriyenko, Sergei 144
Kirov, Sergei 58–9, 101
Kirov ballet company 106
Kolchak, Alexander 44
Komsomol 66
Korea 25, 91, 92, 108,
    119
Kornilov, Lavr 37, 44
Korolev, Sergei 107
Kosygin, Alexei 96, 112
Kovalchuk, Mikhail 155
Kovalchuk, Yuri 155
Kozyrev, Andrei 145, 146
Krasnov, Pyotr 44
kulaks 63
Kurchatov, Igor 92
Kurdistan 31
Kursk Bulge, Battle of 86
Kuwait 132
Kuznetsov, Alexei 95
Kvashnin, Anatoly 149
Kyrgyzstan 16, 17, 159

Labour government, Britain
    73
Land Question 21
Latin America 109
Latvia 16, 42, 79, 80, 133
League of Nations 73

legal system 158
  see also judiciary
Lend-Lease program 85,
  89–90, 93
Lenin
  Bolsheviks 33, 36, 38–40,
    47
  as Communist federalist 55
  death of 57, 59
  Finland 36–7
  as internationalist 55
  leadership 52–3
  mausoleum 68
  peaceful coexistence 72
  sanctity of 102
  Soviet Russian regime 41
  and Stalin 55
  succession 181
  visual arts 68–9
  wounded 43
Lenin in 1918 68
Lenin in October 68
Leningrad 59, 67, 80, 86, 95
  see also Petrograd; St
    Petersburg
Leontief, Vasily 75
Levitan, Isaak 24
Liaodong Peninsula 25
Libya 170
life expectancy 138
Life for the Tsar (Glinka) 71
literacy levels 65
literature 55, 65, 68–9, 75,
  105, 124, 164
Lithuania
  deportees 80
  Germany 30
  and Poland 4

in Russian Empire 16
secession 133
sovereignty 42
Soviet sphere of influence
  79
Litvinenko, Alexander 167
Litvinov, Maxim 74
living standards 104, 136
loans for shares auctions 137
Los Angeles Olympics 117
Luzhkov, Yuri 149–50, 156
Lyubimov, Yuri 115

Magnitsky Act 170
Malenkov, Georgi 96, 100
Malevich, Konstantin 24
Mali 109–10
Malta summit 131–2
Manchuria 16
Mandelstam, Osip 69
Mao Zedong 111
Marshall Plan 93
Marx, Karl 40
Marxism 51, 52, 55, 65, 72
Mayakovsky, Vladimir 68–9
Medvedev, Dmitry 160, 161,
  168
Membership Action Plan,
  NATO 168
Memorial 125
Men, Alexander 115
Mendeleev, Dmitry 24
Mensheviks 27, 40–1
Merezhkovsky, Dmitri 23–4
meritocracy 178
middle class 158–9, 161
Middle East 109, 132, 174
Mikhail, Grand Duke 34

Mikhoels, Solomon 96
military forces 13, 62, 107–8,
    142, 171–2
Miller, Alexei 155
Miller, Yevgeny 44
miners' strikes 127
Minsk 86, 173
Moldova 16, 84, 86, 128, 130
Molotov (Perm) 67
Molotov, Vyacheslav 74,
    78–9, 82, 96, 100, 108
monarchists 32–3
Mongolia 4, 6, 16
monuments 68, 102
morals 49, 98–9, 121
Moscow
    Bolotnaya Square 161, 163
    as capital 43, 95
    Dubrovka Theater 154
    explosions 149
    Orthodox Christianity 5, 6
    redesigned 68
    world youth festival 106
Moscow Art Theater 23
Moscow Olympics 117, 172
Munich Agreement 74, 77
Munich Security Conference
    167
Muscovy 7, 8
Muslim world 6, 9–10, 17
    see also Islamism

Nabokov, Vladimir 75
Nagorno-Karabakh 128, 141
Napoleon Bonaparte 7–8, 31
national anthem 56, 85, 162
nationalism 17, 55, 128–9,
    140

NATO 92, 108, 146, 165–6,
    167–8, 169–70
Navalny, Alexei 163
Nazi Germany 76, 77, 88–9
Neizvestny, Ernst 106
Nekrasov, Nikolai 23
NEP (New Economic Policy)
    53, 61
nerve-gas poisonings 175
Nevsky, Alexander 5, 184
New Economic Policy (NEP)
    53, 61
"new political thinking" 131
Nicaragua 132
Nicholas II, Tsar
    absolute monarch 17–18,
        19, 48
    killed 43, 48
    Korea 25
    leadership 8
    manifesto 27
    Petrograd 34
    Poland 31
    Russian Empire 179
    state funeral 147
Nixon, Richard 116
Nizhny Novgorod (Gorky) 68
NKID (People's Commissariat
    for Foreign Affairs) 72,
    90
nomenklatura 58–9, 102, 112,
    113, 126, 129–30
non-governmental
    organizations 125, 163,
    167
Non-Proliferation Treaty
    116
Norilsk Nickel 137

Normandy landings 86
Novocherkassk protests 105
Novorossiya 173
Novy Mir 105
nuclear arms 92–3, 108–9,
    119, 130, 131, 146
nuclear powerplant explosion
    123
nuclear test ban treaty 110
    see also SALT

Obama, Barack 169, 171
Octoberists 27
Octoberists, children's
    organization 66
OGPU (Chekah) 54
oil sector 144, 157, 158
Okudzhava, Bulat 115
oligarchs 137, 141, 148,
    150–1, 155, 183
*One Day in the Life of Ivan
    Denisovich* (Solzhenisovich)
    64–5, 105, 107
Orlova, Lyubov 69
Orthodox Christianity 3, 4, 5,
    6, 11, 17, 23
    see also Russian Orthodox
    Church
Ossetia, North 154
Ossetia, South 141, 146, 168,
    169
Ottoman Turks 6
Our Savior's cathedral 70,
    162–3

Pamyat 125
Pasternak, Boris 69, 106
patriarchs 6–7, 18, 90–1

patriotism 70, 83–4, 115,
    162, 175
Patrushev, Nikolai 155
Pavlov, Ivan 24
peasantry
    agricultural laborers
    75–6
    collectivization 12, 63–5
    migrations 28
    revolution 26, 53
    serfdom 19–21
    Whites 47
pensions 64, 104, 136,
    158–9, 176
People's Commissariat for
    Foreign Affairs (NKID)
    72, 90
perestroika 14, 120, 122,
    123–6
Perm (Molotov) 67
Pershing II missiles 119
Persia 16, 30
Peter I, Tsar 7, 18
Petrograd 33–4, 35
    see also Leningrad; St
    Petersburg
plane explosions 154
Podgorny, Nikolai 112
poetry 105
Poland
    Brest-Litovsk 41
    Germany 30, 42, 79, 81
    independence 45
    Lithuania 4
    Nicholas II 31
    Red Army 78, 79, 86
    in Russian Empire 16,
    17

Solidarity movement 117
as Soviet satellite 79, 91
Stalin 87–8
Time of Troubles 7
Warsaw Pact 109
police violence 171
Polish–Lithuanian
    Commonwealth 4
Politburo 60, 112, 113, 118,
    123–4
political freedom 26, 147
political prisoners 124
politics/economics 180,
    181–2
Politkovskaya, Anna 167
Ponzi schemes 136
Popkov, Pyotr 95
Popov, Alexander 24
Popov, Gavriil 127
population 17, 20, 28, 47,
    118, 136
    see also ethnic diversity
Port Arthur 16, 91
Potanin, Vladimir 137
Potemkin mutiny 26–7
Potsdam conference 88
poverty 136, 158
POWs (prisoners of war) 42,
    97
Prigozhin, Ilya 75
Primakov, Yevgeny 144, 146,
    149–50
prison population 64–5
privatization 136–7.135
productivity 28, 61, 64,
    118
Progressive Bloc 32
proletariat 39

propaganda 1, 66, 68, 69,
    81, 114
property ownership 28, 75,
    137, 157–8, 160, 182
protests 161, 163
Provisional Government
    35–8
Prussia 16, 30, 91
Pushkin, Alexander 23, 71
Putin, Vladimir
    Chechnya 149, 153–4, 155
    China 174
    economic rehabilitation
        156–8
    election 150, 153, 161
    elites 15, 155–6, 172
    legacy 179, 180–1
    loyalty 144–5
    and Medvedev 160, 161
    NATO 165–6
    oligarchs 150–1
    power 49–50, 153, 154–6
    as pragmatist 176
    Russian Federation 151–2
    social transformation
        158–60
    state capitalism 14–15,
        157–8, 164
    as symbol of patriotism 175
    Ukraine 172, 173, 175
    and USA 182

Radio Liberty 124–5
Rakhmaninov, Sergei 75
Rapallo agreement 72
Rasputin, Grigori 32–3
Reagan, Ronald 131
Realpolitik 72

Red Army
  Bessarabia 75, 86
  Bulgaria 86
  Communist Party 44–5
  Crimea 45
  Finland 80
  Germany 78, 88
  Poland 78, 79, 86
  renamed 90
  Romania 78, 86
  Slovakia 86
  Trotsky 44–5
  victory 47–8
  Wehrmacht 84
Red Guards 36–7, 38
Red Terror 43, 101
regional barons 148, 151
religious faith
  Bolsheviks 70
  centrality of 10
  elites 19
  erosion of 19, 49
  Khrushchev against
    106–7
  Men 115
  Muslim 6
  resurgence 94, 147
  revival 147
  see also Russian Orthodox
    Church
renaming of cities 67–8, 102
renaming of streets 68
Repentance (Abuladze) 124
Repin, Ilya 24
repression 64–5, 93–7,
    101–2, 113
revolutionary consciousness
    39, 61

revolutions
  land reapportioned 21
  1905 26–8
  1917, February 34, 49
  1917, October 27, 46, 66
  peasants 26, 53
  Provisional Government
    35–6
  socialist 27, 40–1
  spiritual sources 11–12
  Ukraine 159, 166
  world 71
Reykjavik summit 131
Ribbentrop, Joachim von
    78–9
Roadside Picnic (Strugatsky
    brothers) 105
Roman Catholicism 4
Romania
  Bessarabia 42, 45, 80
  Red Army 78, 86
  suing for peace 87
  and USSR 88, 91
  Warsaw Pact 109
Romanov dynasty 7, 12, 19
Romm, Mikhail 68
Roosevelt, Franklin D. 73,
    85, 87
Rosneft 155, 157
Rostropovich, Mstislav 114
Rozhdestvensky. Robert 105
RSFSR (Russian Soviet
    Federative Socialist
    Republic) 41
Russia 2–3
  as absolute monarchy
    17–18
  Brest-Litovsk treaty 41–2

elites 160
European Union 166, 167
famine 64
foreign investment 137–8
France 29, 30
Georgia 168–9
Germany 29–30, 72, 73
global role 184–5
India 174
international institutions 46
living standards 136
as Marxist utopia 51
NATO 169–70
nuclear weapons 146
post-Putin 180–2
post-Soviet 135
Syria 170–1
USA 9, 13, 164–7, 169, 182–3
USSR 128–9
Western view of 167
A Russia That We Lost (Govorukhin) 124
Russian Communist Party 127
Russian Empire 7–8, 16–18, 34
  Communist Party 54–5
  Eastern Europe 5, 7
  foreign policy 24–6
  Nicholas II 179
  USSR 80
Russian Federation
  China 174, 183
  constitutional reforms 139–40
  as continuation 8, 11

disintegration threatened 148
economic reforms 135
extent of 16, 54–5
in future 183–5
Mongols 4
Putin 151–2
Ukraine 54
USSR 138
Russian Orthodox Church
  Bolsheviks 43
  Gorbachev 125
  revival 90, 147, 162–3
  Stalin 85
  Synod 18–19
Russian Railways 157
Russian Soviet Federative Socialist Republic (RSFSR) 41
Rutskoi, Alexander 139
Ryazanov, Eldar 115
Rykov, Alexei 59

Saakashvili, Mikheil 168
St Petersburg 2, 7, 29, 31
  see also Leningrad; Petrograd
Sakharov, Andrei 92, 114, 115, 124, 126–7
SALT (strategic arms limitation talks) 116
samizdat copies 107
sanctions 117, 180
Sberbank 158
Schlieffen Plan 30
school hostages 154
science fantasy novels 105
scientific advances 103

scientific exchanges 106
Sechin, Igor 155
secret police 39, 54
self-enrichment 21–2, 180
separatism 56, 142–3, 148, 149, 155
serfdom 19–21, 63–4
Sevastopol 90
Shalamov, Varlam 65
Shaliapin, Feodor 24
Shaymiev, Mintimer 143
Shevardnadze, Eduard 130
Shoigu, Sergei 150, 155
Sholokov, Mikhail 69
Short Course of the History of the All-Union Communist Party 67
Shostakovich, Dmitri 94
shuttle traders 136
Siberia 43, 44, 62, 80, 83–4
Sibneft 137
Sikorsky, Igor 75
Silver Age culture 12, 23, 24
Slovakia 86
Snowden, Edward 171
Sobchak, Anatoly 127, 145
social benefits 159
social justice 74–5
social mobility 67
social transformation 158–60
socialism 12, 27, 40–1, 51–2, 61–3
socialist realism 12, 69
Solidarity movement 117
Solovki prison 54
Solovyov, Vladimir 23
Solzhenitsyn, Alexander 94, 107, 114, 115

The Gulag Archipelago 65, 124
In the First Circle 65
One Day in the Life of Ivan Denisovich 64–5, 105, 107
Soviet Union: *see* USSR
Soviet–German non-aggression pact 78–9
Soviet–German war 85
Spain 73
spies 92
sports 106
Sputnik 103
Stalin (Varna) 102
Stalin, Josef
anti-fascism 73, 96
Baltic States 78
Cold War 92
Communist Party 101
death of 96, 102
as dictator 75–6
"Doctors' Plot" 96
domestic repression 93, 94–5
elites 59, 98
Eurasia 91
Georgia 55, 102
Germany 77–9
Great Patriotic War 84–6, 98
Great Terror 59–60, 101
and Hitler 78, 82
industrialization 61–3
Jewish people 96
legacy of 97–9
and Lenin 55
nuclear weapons 92–3

Poland 87–8
political leadership 57–9,
    60
post-war 90–1
repression 97, 101–2
Roosevelt and Churchill 87
Russian Orthodox Church
    85
socialist economy 61–3
succession 96, 100, 181
and Trotsky 57–8
Stalingrad (Tsaritsyn/
    Volgograd) 67, 90, 102
Stalingrad battle 86
Stalino (Donetsk) 102
Stalker (Tarkovsky) 105
Stanislavsky, Konstantin 23
START treaty 169
state capitalism 157–8, 164,
    183
State of Emergency Committee
    133
State Planning Committee
    (Gosplan) 62
Stolypin, Pyotr 27–8, 29
strategic arms limitation talks
    (SALT) 116
Strategic Rocket Force 107
Stravinsky, Igor 75
strikes 26–7
Strugatsky, Arkady and Boris
    105
subsidies 56, 109
Suez crisis 109
Supreme Soviet 60, 127,
    128–9, 138
Surikov, Vasily 24
Surkov, Vladislav 162

Suslov, Mikhail 115
Sweden 7
Syria 170–1, 174, 175

Taganka Theater 115
Tajikistan 16, 146
tanks 86
Tarkovsky, Andrei 105
Tatarstan 143, 149
Tblisi 168
Tehran conferences 87
television 125
Tereshkova, Valentina 103
terrorism 142–3, 154, 165
terrorist organizations 22, 26,
    27–8
Third World 110
Tikhon, Patriarch 70
Timchenko, Gennady 155
Time of Troubles 7, 8, 50,
    177
Tito, Josip Broz 111
Tolstoy, Leo 23
totalitarianism 12, 13, 49,
    124–5, 177
tourism 106
Transcaucasus Federation 54
Transnistria 146
Trans-Siberia railroad 25
Trasneft 157
Trotsky, Lev 36–7, 39, 41,
    44–5, 55, 57–8
Truman, Harry S. 88
Trump, Donald 174
tsardom 6, 19–20
tsarism 48–9
Tsaritsyn (Stalingrad/
    Volgograd) 67

Tsiolkovsky, Konstantin 23
Tsoi, Viktor 135
Tsvetaeva, Marina 70
Tukhachevsky, Mikhail 60
Turgenev, Ivan 23
Turkestan 16, 42
Turkey 16, 30, 73
Turkic khanates 6, 17
Turkmenistan 16
Tvardovsky, Alexander 105
Tver (Kalinin) 68

Udaltsov, Sergei 163
Ukraine 2, 4
  Brest-Litovsk 17
  Chernobyl explosion 123
  Crimea 112
  deaths in conflicts 173
  energy exports 146
  European Union 171
  famine 64
  foreign policy 164
  Germans driven out 86
  independent state 42, 134
  Kievan Rus 3, 7
  NATO 167–8
  nuclear weapons 146
  police violence 171
  Putin 172, 173, 175
  revolution 159, 166
  Russian Empire 16
  Russian Federation 54
  Wehrmacht 84
Ulyanov, Vladimir: see Lenin
Uncle Vanya (Chekhov) 20
unemployment 125, 136
Union of Right Forces 152
Union of Russian People 27

Union of Soviet Socialist
    Republics: see USSR
United Aircraft 157
United Energy Systems 157
United Nations 88
United Russia 152, 161
United Shipbuilding 157
United States of America
  Afghanistan 165
  Georgia 168–9
  global role 184
  missiles in Europe 116
  nuclear weapon attack on
      Japan 92
  Putin 182
  Russia 9, 13, 164–7, 169,
      182–3
  2016 elections 174
  USSR 73, 85, 116
  Vietnam war 116
Unity coalition 150
university education 66–7
Urals, southern 64
USSR (Union of Soviet
    Socialist Republics) 11,
    54–7
  authoritarianism 13
  Axis powers 82
  Bessarabia 88, 91
  China 73–4, 91, 111, 117,
      132
  as confederation 133
  in crisis 14, 95, 117–20,
      133–4
  Czechoslovakia 73
  decolonization 109
  Eastern Europe 73, 78, 79,
      87, 131

foreign policy 71–4
France 73
Germany 76, 77, 78–80,
    82–4, 108
Hitler 81–2
Japan 73–4, 108
military force 78, 138
movement of heavy
    industry 83–4
patriotism 83–4
religious faith 10
Russia 128–9
Russian Empire 80
Russian Federation 138
satellites 91
secession rights 56, 57
Spain 73
sphere of influence 82
UN Security Council 88
USA 73, 85, 116
Uzbekistan 16

Varna (Stalin) 102
Vekhi (Milestones) 23
Vernardsky, Vladimir 23
Versailles peace conference
    46, 72
Victory Day 88, 89, 94
Vietnam, North 91
Vietnam war 116
Vilnius demonstration
    129–30
visual arts 68–9
Vladivostok 25
Voice of America 124–5
Volga region 43, 64
Volgograd (Stalingrad/
    Tsaritsyn) 102, 149

Voloshin, Alexander 153
voluntarism 111–12
Volunteer Army 44
Voronezh 90
Voznesensky, Andrei 105,
    106
Voznesensky, Nikolai 95
VTB 158
VTB-24 158
Vysotsky, Vladimir 115

war communism 52–3
Warsaw Pact 109, 117
wartime experiences 93–4
wealth 159
wealth redistribution 182
Wehrmacht 83, 84, 86
welfare state 115
Western response 32–3,
    45–6, 91–2
The White Guard (Bulgakov)
    45
Whites 43–4, 45, 46, 47
Winter Palace coup 26, 38
Winter War, Finland 80
Witte, Sergei 27
Women's rights 66
Workers' and Peasants' Red
    Army 44
workers of the world 55
workers' protest, Berlin 109
Workers' Question 21
working conditions 104
World Bank 138
World Economic Forum 141
World War I 12, 28, 29–31,
    33
World War II 13, 77–8, 89

world youth festival 106
Wrangel, Pyotr 45
Writers' Union 69

Yabloko 152
Yakovlev, Alexander 124, 130
Yalta conference 87
Yanukovych, Viktor 164, 172
Yaroslavl 43
Yeltsin, Boris
  Chechnya 142
  constitution 138–40, 142
  elections 127, 138, 140–1
  family 137, 150, 156
  and Gorbachev 95, 126,
    129–30, 133, 135, 156
  health failing 143–4

national referendum 139
  resignation 150
  successors 144–5
Yesenin, Sergei 69, 105
Yevtushenko, Yevgeny 105,
  111
Young Pioneers 66
Yudenich, Nikolai 44
Yugoslavia 111
Yukos oil company 137, 151,
  157, 166

Zhirinovsky, Vladimir 140
Zhukov, Georgy 94, 100
Zinoviev, Grigory 58, 59
Zvorykin, Vladimir 75
Zyuganov, Gennady 140, 141